THE VICTORIAN NOVEL DREAMS OF THE REAL

THE VICTORIAN NOVEL
DREAMS OF THE REAL

Conventions and Ideology

Audrey Jaffe

OXFORD
UNIVERSITY PRESS

OXFORD

UNIVERSITY PRESS

Oxford University Press is a department of the University of Oxford. It furthers the University's objective of excellence in research, scholarship, and education by publishing worldwide. Oxford is a registered trade mark of Oxford University Press in the UK and certain other countries.

Published in the United States of America by Oxford University Press
198 Madison Avenue, New York, NY 10016, United States of America.

Library of Congress Cataloging-in-Publication Data
Names: Jaffe, Audrey.
Title: The Victorian novel dreams of the real : conventions and ideology / Audrey Jaffe.
Description: New York : Oxford University Press, 2016. | Includes bibliographical references.
Identifiers: LCCN 2015030187 | ISBN 978–0–19–026993–7 (cloth) | ISBN 978–0–19–006781–6 (paper) | ISBN 978–0–19–026994–4 (updf)
Subjects: LCSH: English fiction—19th century—History and criticism. | Realism in literature.
Classification: LCC PR878.R4 J34 2016 | DDC 823/.80912—dc23 LC record available at http://lccn.loc.gov/2015030187

CONTENTS

CONTENTS

ACKNOWLEDGMENTS

The English Department at the University of Toronto provided a stimulating and congenial atmosphere in which to think about, teach, and discuss these ideas over the past few years. Jill Matus and Cannon Schmitt helpfully commented on individual chapters, and the interest and energy of students in my graduate seminars kept me going. Kirsten Hainer in particular has been a true pal: generous with her comments and unshakeable in her enthusiasm. Nancy Armstrong was a willing friend at a crucial moment, and I am happy to acknowledge here how much I have learned from and been influenced by her work.

It has been a pleasure to discuss this material with audiences and seminar participants at a number of venues, including, at the University of Toronto, WINCS (Work in Nineteenth-Century Studies), expertly directed by Terry Robinson and Mark Knight, and the organizers of the Brown Bag talks. My thanks also to the Victorian Studies Association of Ontario; the North American Victorian Studies Association; the English Department at the University of Missouri, Columbia; the Nineteenth-Century Colloquium at the University of California, Berkeley; the Victorian Studies Institute, and the Philadelphia-area Nineteenth-Century Studies group. Among those I have met at these sites and others I want to single out Sarah Winter, Peter Logan, Kent Puckett, Rachel Buurma and Matthew Rowlinson for their willingness to discuss these ideas. Readers for Oxford University Press offered expert guidance in the revision process, as did editor Brendan O'Neill, and I thank them all for their careful attention. I owe special thanks to Stephen Bradley and Deepti Agarwal for their responsiveness and helpfulness during the book's production. An earlier version of chapter 4 appeared in *Novel* 43 (2010), 381–400.

There would be no book ever without the invaluable support, brilliant insights, and necessary course corrections of Mary Ann O'Farrell and Peter Schwartz.

THE VICTORIAN NOVEL DREAMS OF THE REAL

Introduction

Realist Fantasy

[I]f what we experience as "reality" is structured by fantasy, and if fantasy serves as the screen that protects us from being directly overwhelmed by the raw Real, then *reality itself can function as an escape from encountering the Real.* In the opposition between dream and reality, fantasy is at the side of reality, and it is in dreams that we encounter the traumatic Real.

Slavoj Žižek, "Psychoanalysis and the Lacanian Real"

For weeks, for months, if I remember rightly, from year to year, I would carry on the same tale, binding myself to certain laws, to certain proportions and proprieties, and unities. . . . I learned in this way to maintain an interest in a fictitious story, to dwell on a work created by my own imagination, and to live in a world altogether outside the world of my own material life. In after years I have done the same,—with this difference, that I have discarded the hero of my early dreams, and have been able to lay my own identity aside.

Anthony Trollope, An Autobiography

What does it mean to position the real "at the side" of—or in the same place as—fantasy?

Including that which we cannot understand and therefore (he argues) cannot face in the category of the "raw Real," Žižek, following

Lacan, aligns the ordinary, everyday real with what he calls fantasy. Anthony Trollope, in a process he described as training for the writing of realist novels, combines the two modes in a series of daydreams that effectively become those novels, allowing him to realize his dream of becoming a celebrated author. Leaving aside for the moment the status of Žižek's third term, the capitalized Real (except to note that the claim that its location is known—that, however inaccessible, it can be identified—is a key element of the fantasy I address in this book), I want to discuss here the overlapping of fantasy with the real in Victorian fiction. I argue that the "real," for the Victorian novelists who seek to represent and capture it, is an object of desire and is therefore, necessarily, a fantasy. Calling the real into being for characters and readers through the use of specific conventions, these novelists produce what I call *realist fantasy*. The conventions they deploy to produce the real, as they imagine it, move in and out of perception, simultaneously inviting and excluding both characters and readers: soliciting participation even as they suggest its impossibility. These conventions, moreover, structure the individual fantasies, dreams, daydreams, and desires of characters in a manner that highlights the fantasmatic nature of Victorian realism itself. Another way of saying this, as my title suggests, is that it is not only characters, but the novels they inhabit, that dream of the real.[1]

It is, of course, a post-structuralist truism to say that realism can only gesture toward the real: that realist effects, as Roland Barthes calls them, are the result of conventions, and that such structures carry with them a host of ideological imperatives.[2] Despite this, criticism of the Victorian realist novel remains, and, indeed, has in recent years become increasingly attached to, the idea of a real behind realism, as attested to by recent methodological turns, including New Historicism (itself a response to deconstruction's abstraction); thing theory, and surface reading—expressions of realist desire I address in my conclusion. Realism's desire for the real has not typically been part of this discussion, nor has the way in which, if realism is a function of desire, the conventions that structure it necessarily overlap with those of the fantasy or dream states to which it is frequently opposed, and which it often—both structurally and thematically—renders the target of its own critique.

This book aligns Victorian novelistic realism with the Victorians' overarching desire, both cultural and ideological, for the real. It is realism's particular magic, I argue—and here I borrow a description of Trollope's realism from Walter Kendrick—to enable us to see the conventions it uses and not see them at the same time: to perceive the illusory nature of the structures that, as Žižek puts it, shape "our effective, real social relations" and nevertheless treat them as realities.[3] Realist fiction shares this doubleness with the real itself—those structures, both material and ideological, that shaped everyday life for the Victorians and that shape our daily experience as well: structures to whose "reality" we must, however provisionally, consent. This consent makes it possible to suggest that not only realism but also what we call the real is a genre, a system of rules with its own decipherable codes and conventions—conventions whose realist effects resemble, and may be said to rely on and to some extent derive from, the fictions that are said to imitate them.[4] The book rereads many of the conventions that have been used to define and analyze realist fiction—including metonymy; the use of the detail; an emphasis on the empirical and the visual; the idea of disillusionment and that of consensus. And it also describes the way in which an author's use of particular conventions—conventions unique to particular novels—structures individual characters' fantasies and shapes the more general and generalized fantasies that constitute each novel's imagining of the real. I argue that realism and fantasy in these novels occupy the same space and are constructed via the same conventions, which, failing to distinguish the object of knowledge from the object of desire, invite readers to do the same.

That the nineteenth century more generally shared the realist novel's dream is signaled by such familiar formulations as Matthew Arnold's definition of culture as the ability to "see things as they really are." It is manifested as well in the strains of thought traced by Lorraine Daston and Peter Galison in their history of Victorian objectivity, especially their account of "mechanical objectivity," which, they argue, sought to do away with any human mediation or "tampering" with scientific images so that those images could "print themselves on the page"; and, as well, in what Rhonda Batchelor has referred to as "the Victorians' near-fetishization of the quotidian for its apparent stability."[5] My contention that there was a general nineteenth-century desire for the real draws as well on the way the structure of Victorian ideologies—about domesticity, character, and gender, among other things—supports the Althusserian account of ideology as an "imaginary relationship to the real conditions of existence," with the term "imaginary" defined not as an escape from the real but rather *as* the real, insofar as that is the name given to the institutions and structures that make up the social world.[6] The point of this formulation is that the imaginary and the real are indistinguishable from one another, and that ideology is made manifest in—invested with reality by—the world of things, structures, and institutions. Material and spatial constructions that simultaneously invite and exclude—literal "frames" such as windows and doorways and the structure of the home—are themselves seductively "real"-seeming ideological forms. Such constructions, that is, locate the real in the manifestations of substance and solidity the Victorians prized—manifestations that continue to dominate critical theories of realist fiction. Indeed, the ideological investments of a desire for the real are embedded in the phrase Daston and Galison use to describe the nineteenth-century pursuit of objectivity: "epistemic virtue" (16).

It is not my contention that nineteenth-century novelists agreed—either with scientists or with one another—about the nature of the real, or that they wished to erase all traces of the perceiver or knower from their representations. Indeed, George Eliot famously writes in the manifesto that makes up the seventeenth chapter of *Adam Bede* of her effort to give a "faithful account of men and things as they have mirrored themselves in my mind."[7] My point is rather that there is a basic agreement between nineteenth-century epistemological history on the one hand, and Althusserian/Lacanian ideological theory on the other, that the object of knowledge and the object of desire coalesce in an idea or fantasy of the real (and in this sense, there is no contradiction between a desire to represent an objective external reality and Eliot's notion of faithfulness: both rely on an ideal of accurate representation). And they coalesce, as well, in the form of novels that, by means of various representational strategies, take on the task of reproducing or capturing it. To the extent that novels and the critical tradition that seeks to classify and characterize them have both endorsed a realism that consists of, for example, repeated and recognizable elements; the evocation of solid material realities; a recognizable, habitual linearity of space and time; unique and coherent characters possessing depth or interiority and, thematically, an emphasis on disillusionment (or what I refer to here as pre-disillusionment)—and I am listing here only the most commonly agreed-upon features said to define realist fiction—they have mutually assisted in the construction of a fantasy of the real.[8] The consolidation of realism as a genre—to some extent during the Victorian period itself, and to some extent later, within literary criticism—is itself one result of this agreement. Realism in this book is thus not fantasy's alternative, as the usual generic distinctions would have it, but rather its fulfillment.

In the novels I discuss here, some but not all generally considered part of the realist canon (though the existence of such a canon, as I discuss below, is not a settled issue), specific conventions function as frameworks for the novel's realism. But these conventions also appear in the individual fantasies, dreams, and daydreams of the novel's characters, as if to suggest that realist ideology and individual fantasy have to overlap in order for realist dreams to come true. The larger forms these realist dreams take, I propose, are the novels themselves, which may be seen both as projections of a more general desire for the real—an instance of a phenomenon on display throughout the nineteenth century—and as a specific novelist's own realist fantasy: the terms and conventions by means of which Eliot, Trollope, Dickens, Hardy, and Collins imagine the real. My goal, then, is not an unmasking of realist representation as representation, or the defining of a certain set of conventions as the genre's *sine qua non*, but rather a reconceptualization of novelistic realism as a mapping of what these novels represent as the real onto what they also depict as fantasy.[9] Realist novels, in sum—and novels that are not classified as realist, but make use of realist conventions, such as Collins's *Armadale*—represent not the real but the desire for it, and in doing so render it desirable for readers as well.

I have chosen for this book novels that represent a variety of approaches to the realist project and various forms of realist desire, from the self-proclaimed representational and ideological—what I call the spectacular—realism of Eliot's *Adam Bede*, to novels that have been called both realist and non-realist (*Oliver Twist* and *The Mayor of*

Casterbridge, as well as several other of Hardy's novels), to works that transcend an explicitly realist framework and deliberately challenge realism's boundaries (*Armadale*). The emphasis throughout is less on revisiting an established canon or devising a new one than on the way these novels highlight their own use of realist conventions—both those familiar from accounts in realist theory, and those unique to specific texts. Thus *Oliver Twist* and *Mayor* are here because they use coincidence in ways that produce both realist and non-realist effects, while Trollope's *Orley Farm* enables a discussion of (among other issues) Trollope's opposition—in the name of realism—to what he describes as the withholding strategies of sensation fiction. That novel also articulates what I see as realist fantasy's intertwined thematics of invitation and prohibition in the question within which its daydreaming characters frame their own fantasies: why should I not? Hardy's *The Return of the Native* enables a discussion of the framing of realist space as exclusive rather than wholly inclusive, and a rereading of metonymy as the figure that facilitates its functioning as such, so that a character's or person's surroundings become a kind of enclosure for personality, a boundary between the self and others. And *Armadale*—not considered realist by its author or its readers—parodies realist conventions even as, I suggest, it expresses a desire for the real.

This book thus considers what I call realist fantasy as it takes shape on several different levels: that of individual characters, as they dream and desire; of particular novelists, as they imagine the real; of the construction of realism as a genre; and of Victorian culture as refracted through its ideological imperatives: those conventions that structure novelistic realism and those similarly arbitrary and often unarticulated rules that structure the social real. My use of the term "fantasy" refers to individual/psychological categories, literary classifications, and ideological institutions and discourses—categories which, of course, overlap with one another—and in all these contexts it is meant to shift the critical conversation about the Victorian realist novel away from the assumption of cohesiveness the term "realist" suggests (the attempt to define realism or the realist novel) and toward the way realist fiction and its critics manifest a desire to claim the real—as territory, to use my name for *Adam Bede*'s sealing off of realist space.[10] I am not concerned with saying what realism "is," but rather with the idea that novels desire something they define as the real, and that any authority they claim for a particular way of seeing things is founded on this desire.

What builds realist territory, and mediates between individual fantasies and a novel's more general ones, are conventions: devices that frame a novel's reality both for individual characters and for the novels in which we find them. My purpose is partly to reread what have become in the critical canon "classic" realist conventions, such as metonymy in Jakobson's definition or the realist detail in Barthes's. But it is also to expand the idea of convention itself to include the different ways in which each novel constructs its version of the real: conventions that both enable characters' fantasies and make up the more general fantasy that constitutes a novel's imagining of the real. All of these novels, that is, in some way take on traditional realist conventions—most prominently the solid materiality of persons and things and the singularity or specialness of realist character—simultaneously endorsing them as real and framing them as fantasy. And they also introduce conventions of their own: idiosyncratic forms used to shape a novel's specific reality. In doing so the novels extend to readers the same invitation they extend to characters, positioning us in a seductive and yet impossible-to-fulfill relation to a fantasized real.

"Realism" has long been a vexed term for those who write about and teach it. Though several authors of nineteenth-century British fiction explicitly thought of themselves as realists and discussed what they meant by the term—Eliot and Trollope in particular—there is no self-defined school of English realism and no consensus about which authors and texts must be included in any discussion of it. References to "the realists" seem misguided, since the phrase suggests a self-constituted collection of authors with similar values and aims, and in England there was no such group.[11] Dickens is sometimes included, especially for the disillusionment plot of *Great Expectations*; George Gissing's bleak renderings of late-century topical conditions, and especially his critique of realism in *New Grub Street*, often provide a helpful endpoint. Other novelists who might fit the bill, such as Arnold Bennett, arrive later in the century and tend to be classified as naturalists; Trollope, perhaps the likeliest of the mid-century candidates, is less-frequently taught than Eliot, Dickens, and Brontë because of the novels' length: a discursiveness he and others have described as a key element of their realism.[12]

Ian Watt's influential argument (1957), that the realist novel in England emerged alongside empiricism and the growth of the middle class, was grounded in the form's evocation of ordinary lives and material details, as well as in representations of causality and linear time that aligned "commonsensical" (Weinstein 276) experience with novelistic constructions of time and space, has been critiqued and expanded but not substantially overridden; writes Peter Brooks in 2005, introducing his argument about the visual construction of the real in the nineteenth-century novel, "[T]o work through the accumulation of things, of details, of particularities, could be considered nearly definitional of the realist novel." Roman Jakobson's linguistic account of metonymy and metaphor, written earlier but only widely circulated later, reinforced that argument, tying realism to the representation of ordinary, non-symbolic objects and to linearity and narrative. Roland Barthes's essay on realist representation focused similarly on the depiction of ordinary things, crucially the barometer on the piano in Flaubert's "A Simple Heart," which, he claimed, guaranteed the kind of non-meaning we find in the ordinary world.[13]

The general tenor of these arguments is so persuasive, their "commonsensical" approach so completely aligned with the novels' own articulations of the real, that the circularity of their arguments tends to be overlooked. In the introduction to his book about realism and visuality, for instance, Brooks assimilates realist convention and the real. It may be true in some sense that realism is, as he writes, "a kind of literature and art committed to a form of play that uses carefully wrought and detailed toys, ones that attempt as much as possible to reproduce the look and feel of the real thing," and that in doing so it is chiefly concerned with visuality: with registering the presence of these toys, or things, through sight (3). But what "real thing" is at issue here? And what might be said of fiction such as Trollope's, which is less interested in things—the look and feel of objects—than in thoughts? As soon as Brooks evokes "the real thing," he has moved from a discussion of conventions to an assumption that his conception of the real is generally shared. This happens, I would suggest, because Watt's argument about the rise of empiricism reflects a consensus not only about realist fiction but about the nature of the real in general within this tradition; it describes not just novelistic realism but the codes that constitute a widely-accepted definition of the genre known as the real. Seamlessly aligned with that definition, his emphasis on the empirical, the material, and the ordinary proves irresistible.[14]

Other approaches to realism tend to have in common a project of defining what elements, in any selected series of texts, allow a novel to be characterized as "realist."[15] Sometimes the emphasis is thematic—*Great Expectations*, for instance, with its melodramatic plot and fairy-tale subplot, is often found to be classically realist in its disillusionment of Pip's fantasies; sometimes it is theoretical, as in the case of *Adam Bede*, which tends to be considered an ur-text of British realism largely because of its included manifesto—the famous seventeenth chapter—about the relation between Dutch painting and realist art. In *The Realistic Imagination* (1981), George Levine made Mary Shelley's *Frankenstein*—a text not usually associated with realism—his model for a theory of realist repression, while Leo Bersani's *A Future for Astyanax* (1976) used Austen's *Mansfield Park* to begin a discussion of the way desire disrupts realist character.

Criticism of the Victorian realist novel in recent decades includes, among many other examples, Catherine Belsey's chapter on Althusserian interpellation; Colin MacCabe's essay on the hierarchical discourse of the classic realist text; D. A. Miller's Foucauldian analysis in *The Novel and the Police*; Deidre Lynch's work on character; Alex Woloch's argument about the distribution of attention in realist narrative, and Aaron Matz's discussion of satirical realism. Elizabeth Ermarth has argued that the omniscient narrator of realist fiction relies on an ideal of consensus, while Nancy Armstrong has demonstrated the way novelistic representation is shaped by the rhetoric of photographic images. Elaine Freedgood joined thing theory to historicism, using extra-literary sources to trace the "real" histories of objects to which novels refer, while Elaine Hadley tied realist form to the structure and ethics of nineteenth-century liberal thought, and Richard Menke argued for its links to the circulation of Victorian information. And Fredric Jameson has argued for what he calls the "antinomies" of realism: a distinction between affective content and what he calls "present consciousness."[16]

I am not concerned with the accuracy or comprehensiveness of these arguments, nor is it my goal to dispute them. Rather, I want to point toward the consistent, ongoing, and multifarious interest in and attempts to account for the power of Victorian realism, and a general taking for granted of something that accompanies it: the Victorian realist novel's persistent desire for the real. The continued attempt to define novelistic realism suggests an addition to realism's numerous effects: the way in which realism's very persuasiveness—its apparent purchase on the real—creates a critical version of realist desire, a desire to know how it works. Whatever form that desire takes, however—whatever theory seems, at any given moment, to uncover the secret of its effects—my larger interest is that it exists at all: that the desire to see things one way and not another, whether individual, cultural, or (necessarily) both, tends to require a claim on (or for) the real.[17] Thus even though, like other critics, I have necessarily selected specific texts to illustrate my point, it would contradict my purpose to redefine realism in general, establish a new canon, or make a claim for a particular set of themes. I wish to suggest, instead, that when the novels I discuss here attempt to represent fantasy, dream, or daydream by making use of the conventions on which their own realist representation relies, or when the two modes overlap in the structure of realist conventions, these novels produce what I am calling realist fantasy: a desire for the real that takes shape as a wish, dream, daydream, and, in its most exemplary form, the realist novel itself.

In a dream of the real that can be ascribed to no one in particular, Pierre Bourdieu describes the way symbolic meanings are encoded in ostensibly objective "facts" of the world. Using language that recalls Henri Lefebvre's discussions of space, Bourdieu writes of the way symbolic meanings embodied in the Kabyle house are "read" by the body, so that, for instance, the division into front and back corresponds to differences of gender and status. By way of a certain "magic," he writes, "each thing speaks metaphorically of all the others, each practice comes to be invested with an objective meaning":

> The construction of the world of objects is clearly not the sovereign operation of consciousness which the neo-Kantian tradition conceives of. . . . The mind born of the world of objects does not rise as a subjectivity confronting an objectivity: the objective universe is made up of objects which are the product of objectifying operations structured according to the very structures which the mind applies to it. [18]

As Nancy Armstrong succinctly puts it, "an object is never just an object."[19] In Bourdieu's account, by dint of repetition, reproduction, and the transmutation of imagined effects into physical objects—the structures of the made world—the arbitrary comes to seem inevitable; what appears as the objective "real" is an effect of the investment of meaning in things. It is the realist novel's particular magic, I argue—like that of the glass cover Hawthorne used as an image for Trollope's realism ("just as real as if some giant had hewn a great lump out of the earth and put it under a glass case, with all its inhabitants going about their daily business, and not suspecting they were being made a show of")—to bring what appears to be "just" an object into view as an author (or a culture, or both) wishes it to be seen (and the question begged by the term "just" extends, as I argue in my conclusion, to surface reading's directive that critics should "just read").[20] Framing the real as the result of a wish or desire, realist fiction exposes what Bourdieu calls "the arbitrary content of the culture" (94). As realist effects overlap with dreams, daydreams, and other ostensibly non-realist forms, they at once assimilate a character's fantasies to a necessary reality—one required by genre, and, it seems to follow, by the "real" world that genre helps to reproduce—and reorient readers' relations, in different ways and to different degrees, to the novelistic real.

The chapters that follow conceptualize the relation between fantasy and the real, and more specifically the articulation of the real as fantasy, in several different ways. In some of these examples, a character's particular dream or fantasy is an exemplary version of a scenario the novel enacts on a larger scale: a framed or marked instance of what appears, at the level of the novel's ostensible realism, unframed and unmarked. Such is the case, for instance, in the explicitly non-realist text, Wilkie Collins's *Armadale*, in which the presence of a dreamer serves as the most basic and explicit indication that we are in a dream world rather than a waking one. But in other cases, for instance that of *Adam Bede*, the narrator's realistic account is itself framed in such a way as to make its status as representation apparent and to enhance the desirability of the real it represents: the specific scenario of Adam's fantasy about Dinah's presence in his mother's kitchen, and the framing of Dinah herself as a fantasy of interiority, reinforce the simultaneously ideological and dreamlike status of the realist text. My point is not that the more realist section of a text scapegoats or ejects aspects of another genre in order to affirm the novel's realism—a case that has been persuasively made for *Adam Bede*'s relation to the romance form to which Hetty Sorrel's story seems to belong—but rather that the use of the same conventions in these ostensibly different modes affirms the status of the real as fantasy: what the novel renders desirable through the mechanics of representation. By means of such devices, realist fiction renders the real itself an object of desire.

George Eliot's emphasis on the material reality of *Adam Bede*'s characters and spaces, for instance, is part of that novel's claim on the real. But the conventions Eliot uses to represent that reality simultaneously point toward its unreality: fantasy and the real, as in Trollope's "castles in the air"—his name for the daydreams by means of which he taught himself to write realist fiction—occupy the same space. Thus the apparent solidity of *Adam Bede*'s realist forms is achieved in part by the way Eliot distances readers from them, rendering the real desirable by representing it as spectacle—putting it, in effect, inside Hawthorne's glass case. This framing structure does double duty, pointing simultaneously toward the real and the fantasmatic, demonstrating how the effect that Roland Barthes called "realist" is indeed only an effect. And in several of the novels discussed here, this evocation of framing structures aligns realist representation with more general Victorian ideologies, such as domesticity, as well as with the production of desire characteristic of Victorian spectatorship, as in Hawthorne's description of Trollope's realism. Indeed, these overlap in Hawthorne's account, as Walter Kendrick points out: "The only difference between the world inside and the world outside is the glass." He adds, "there can be no realism unless the reader simultaneously sees the glass and pretends that he does not see it."[21] If we take the glass to signify both the material and ideological enclosures of everyday life—with its inhabitants "going about their daily business, and not suspecting they were being made a show of"— the conventions I discuss here, both general and idiosyncratic, enable us to see them and not see them at the same time.

Dreams and daydreams come into play explicitly when a novel's realist fantasy incorporates the dreams or daydreams of characters, blurring the boundaries between registers by projecting the real not as fantasy's opposite but as its most desired form: what can be dreamt of and also achieved, circumscribed as it is by the rules and prohibitions of social life—as in the desire of Trollope's characters to marry the objects of their affections, or Michael Henchard's desire, in *The Mayor of Casterbridge*, to be mayor. In Eliot's novel, the representation of domestic space discussed above in more abstract terms figures conspicuously in the main character's fantasy. An explicit conflation of daydream and the ideological real characterizes the moment at which Adam Bede imagines hearing Hetty Sorrel (the object of his own fantasy) in his mother's kitchen, but enters to find Dinah Morris (the fulfillment of the novel's fantasy, and of the culture's ideological imperative) instead. In Trollope's *Orley Farm*, similarly, the fantasies of individual characters take shape as a confrontation with prohibitions—social rules and proprieties—in the same way that Trollope regulated his own fantasies in accordance with his idea of realism ("binding myself to certain laws, to certain proportions, and proprieties, and unities"; 144.).

These novels also stage a tension between traditional realist character—possessing the effects of depth, interiority, and individuality that are conventional in realist fiction—and a fungibility or positionality more typical of sensation fiction: that is, the recognition or awareness that a social role (mayor, mother, or orphan boy, for instance) may be held by more than one person, and indeed what often seems to be the necessary priority, in plots frequently involving doubling and duplicity, of position over person. These novels suggest that the distinctiveness of traditional realist character is itself a fantasy, and character itself perhaps something more like a frame for a certain kind of content, as in the substitution of Dinah for Hetty in the role of wife, or the multiply-signifying title "Mayor of Casterbridge."[22] The point is not, however, that one construction of character is more realistic than another, but rather that well before sensation fiction rendered explicit (as Ronald Thomas argues) a shift from "high realist" character to an identity-based model—identity as a matter of textual verification—Victorian novels repeatedly questioned realism's notion of depth, positioning character simultaneously as individualized, on the one hand, and as a framework or vehicle for genre and its accompanying ideologies on the other. In *Oliver Twist* and *The Mayor of Casterbridge*, the central character's singularity or uniqueness—a traditional aspect of novelistic realism—comes up against an equally persuasive reality of nondescriptness; these are reconciled by means of the narrative magic of coincidence, a convention that, I argue, underwrites both realism and fantasy. Realist character turns out to be, simultaneously, ordinary and nondescript as well as the object of fantasy and dream: a combination, we might say, of what the "mass" reader fears about being part of the mass—something like Oliver on the London streets—and how the same reader might imagine escaping that condition. Lost, initially, on the streets, Oliver turns out to be something like a royal personage accidentally misplaced: a beloved family member and the rightful inheritor of ancestral wealth. Hardy, in the novels discussed here, repeatedly stages a character's sense of his own singularity as a fantasy, sustained by the character himself (and reinforced by a novelistic structure that requires a "central" character) and any others who support him in it, but not by the novel's own evocation of place-changing and repetition, in *The Mayor of Casterbridge*, or the positing of uniqueness as shared fantasy in *The Return of the Native*. The plot of Collins's *Armadale* involves the fulfillment of a character's dream, and in this context, I argue, the novel's sensational characters dream of being realist ones. And yet in pointing toward the real (and away from it, as in the novel's use of sensational dreams), both Collins and his characters find only an adherence to or disruption of realist conventions, as character itself serves as a vehicle for mediating differences between genres. Indeed, in the novels I discuss here, a choice of modes or genres is often staged as a choice of fantasies.

Such differences describe the tension in *Oliver Twist* between the improbability of the novel's numerous coincidences, on the one hand, and the use of coincidence to ground realist subjectivity on the other. It appears in the structure of Trollope's authorial fantasies, and in the way *Orley Farm*'s characters—like their author—daydream according to realist conventions, finding themselves not only unable to escape the rules and prohibitions of ordinary life but in fact seeking them out as daydreaming's enabling condition. Hardy's *Return of the Native*, alternatively, challenges the separation of fantasy and the real in the form of characters who, unable to confirm the reality of what they see unless someone else sees it too, explicitly pose the question of whether the real is anything other than (as in Žižek's formulation) shared fantasy. And yet I would argue that this difference in mode—between fantasy, dream, or daydream on the one hand, and realism on the other—is formulated most explicitly as a difference in genre in Collins's *Armadale*: the exemplary non-realist novel I discuss here. *Armadale*'s version of dream theory involves the dreamer's transformation of the mundane details of ordinary life into something more closely resembling the terrors of sensation fiction. That translation, like the influence of Victorian fiction on Freudian interpretation more generally, suggests the possibility that the distinction between consciousness and unconsciousness, as conventionally understood, is analogous to, if not an effect of, the nineteenth century's investment in distinguishing and codifying differences in literary genres, most crucially between realist and sensational forms.[23]

This book seeks to articulate a theory about Victorian realist fiction that does not depend on but rather fleshes out the idea of what "feels real"—since, to refer once again to Žižek on Althusser, the idea of the real is inseparable from that of ideology, and an indication of ideology's success is precisely the feeling of "reality" it conveys.[24] Since I am more interested in how realist effects are achieved than in redefining and relocating the real, I make use of work by theorists whose articulations of the techniques, strategies, and conventions of realist fiction have come to define the classic realist text and tend to be invoked most frequently in discussions of novelistic realism.[25] Barthes's "Reality Effect," for instance, which considers the non-referentiality of detail in the realist text, and Althusser's concepts of ideology and interpellation, which discuss the way certain structures and institutions come to "feel real" or hold the place of the real, when, in Žižek's words, "we do not feel any opposition between it [ideology] and reality" (49), provide a set of terms for describing the structural identity of the ostensibly real and fantasmatic. I make use as well of the idea of metonymy, which Roman Jakobson defined as a key feature of realist fiction. These and other foundational accounts of realism enable the delineation of a particular text's realist fantasy: what it wants from the idea of the real; what kinds of compulsions and beliefs it evokes; what values it assumes and assimilates.

My emphasis on fantasy is in part a response to the recent critical turn toward materiality and the ostensibly real, as manifest in the idea of "surface reading" and a corresponding emphasis on the extraliterary histories of objects. These arguments, drawing on new historical criticism, thing theory, and book history, sometimes seek to provide the objects that circulated in Victorian culture and Victorian fiction with "real" histories of their own. [26] But the accompanying claim that realist fiction represses and conceals the truth of these objects is arguably a shift from the fetishization of novels to that of history, situating objects—also fetishized by this emphasis—within an unmediated reality, one outside cultural narrative, as embodiments of the inarguably real.[27] My approach to the idea of realism thus has more in common with Peter Logan's argument about fetishism than with attempts to delineate the true histories of objects named in novels. Distinguishing between critics who separate the object from its representation, on the one hand, and novelistic realism itself, which seeks to "obscure that distinction" on the other, Logan suggests that "the fetishistic goal of realism—to create an object that succeeds by coming to life—gives it a counterintuitive resemblance to the discourse of fantasy, that narrative mode familiarly hinging on a fetishistic dream."[28] His example of such a dream is *Pinocchio*, the story of the puppet come to life. As he argues, realist fiction both unmasks and shares the reader's tendency to "invest inert objects with an independent existence" (87). To pull apart the object and its representation in order to point toward a more "real" reality, as much recent criticism does, is, I would argue, another way of fetishizing the real, merely resituating the fixedness or solidity of its definition. Indeed, situating real things as a persistent object of desire, this practice illustrates my more general point: whether critics locate the real within the mind of the reader; within textual boundaries; or in a social and/ or historical realm valorized because it is seen as "more" real than fiction, their shared desire to capture or locate it manifests a fascination with the authoritative, grounded status of their object—itself a product and perpetuation of nineteenth-century ideologies.[29] Like Nancy Armstrong in *How Novels Think*, I am more interested in the reality a novel calls into being than in the idea that there is a more real reality outside it.[30] Another way of putting this is to suggest the value of treating realism not only as a literary genre but also as a conceptual framework for understanding the real: not solely as a source for representations but, as Bourdieu suggests, as itself a genre or mode, a system of representational rules.[31]

If we think about the real in this way (a house is never just a house; an object is never just an object), it is not surprising that many Victorian realist novels produce what Ramón Saldivar has called, in a discussion of Trollope, "fantasies about a well-ordered and intelligible society."[32] Because desire requires a structure of exclusion—readers must be situated "outside" the structures designed to evoke their desire—invitation and prohibition in Victorian realist fiction (conventionally paradigmatic qualities of, respectively, fantasy and the real) necessarily take the same form. The site of fantasy is also the site of the real—or, as Lefebvre puts it, the place of yes is also a place of no (204). The regimen of literary labor Trollope imposed on himself, for instance, bound him as a subject, but was also his way of fulfilling a particular dream of self-making. Echoing throughout the daydreams of characters in *Orley Farm*, the phrase "why should I not" opens up the question of how far a character may go in bending or breaking the rules, framing fantasy as a matter of seeking out the prohibitions that may prevent the realization of—but also help produce—fantasy. Realism's "real" thus takes shape in these novels as a regulated fantasy, or what I call in my discussion of *Adam Bede* a fantasy of solidity, in which what is presented as most desirable—and what else is fantasy but the imagining of what one desires?—is what appears to a particular author and, persuasively, to his or her readers as the forms and rules designated as the structure of actual life.

But the story of realist fantasy I am telling is also, as must be apparent by now, the story of a realism that seeks solidity precisely because it fears its absence. It thus makes sense that as realist texts affirm the solidity of their construction, their elaborate defenses and prohibitions, like the doorways and windows that seek to secure the space of the home against external disruptions, also suggest, by way of their openness and transparency, the fragility and instability of these same structures. The conventions I describe operate on both sides of the realist divide, simultaneously demarcating and failing to demarcate boundaries between fantasy and the real. The book may seem to trace a trajectory in which traditional realism is treated with increasing skepticism, and it is indeed the case that Hardy and Collins are the most explicit in framing realism, or any character's particular idea of the real, as fantasy. But this same configuration—a simultaneous seeing and not-seeing of the glass— appears as well in the imagined position of the reader in *Adam Bede*; the use of coincidence in *Oliver Twist*; *The Mayor of Casterbridge*'s system of character substitution, and the Trollopian convention of building castles in the air. Indeed, if *Armadale* seems to offer this book's most self-conscious awareness of genre and of the construction of character as a generic effect, Collins undoes that self-consciousness when he directs readers toward a wholly sensational newspaper account of a ship named *The Armadale*. What feels real at any moment is both tenuous and all one has to go on.

The sense of comfort realism provides in these novels is thus often simultaneously a sense of discomfort. Sometimes, as in *Adam Bede*, this is a way of saying that the rules and prohibitions that characterize the real are, indeed, comfortable—that they are desirable because they are comfortable, and that part of the business of defining the difference between inside and outside, interiority and its absence, lies in constructing the former as desirable: where (and what) one wants to be. But it is also a way of saying that the clear definitions and self-recognitions offered by what might be called "home" conventions—realist conventions—are always provisional: neither demonstrably real nor obviously fantasmatic, but inevitably both at the same time.

I want to return, then, briefly, to the capitalized "Real" used in the epigraph at the head of this introduction. For there is something fetishistic as well about the belief that the capital "R" has the power to summon the idea of a realer real: one more real than the ordinary and unproblematic arena of daily life can offer; one that only the unconscious might encounter, unmediated, in dreams. As I argue in my final chapter with reference to critical attempts to claim the real, there is no better way to assert power than to control the form of discourse, and there is no better way to control discourse than by claiming ownership of the real. Indeed, the inaccessibility of that capital-R "Real" keeps the idea of it in play. The resemblance of this formulation to an experience that, George Eliot suggested, might overwhelm us if we could have it—"if we had a keen vision and feeling of all ordinary life, it would be like hearing the grass grow and the squirrel's heart beat, and we should die of that roar which lies on the other side of silence"—suggests the inarguable quality of (and therein perhaps the best reason for wanting power over) the realist idea: an idea that, like the capital "R," can only be magical or fetishistic, in its apparent capacity to call into being the very reality it claims to have discovered.[33]

Chapter 1

Realist Territory

Invitation and Prohibition in *Adam Bede*

The meanings conveyed by abstract space are more often prohibitions than solicitations or stimuli (except when it comes to
consumption). Prohibition—the negative basis, so to speak, of
the social order—is what dominates here. The symbol of this
constitutive repression is an object offered up to the gaze yet
barred from any possible use, whether this occurs in a museum
or in a shop window. It is impossible to say how often one pauses
uncomfortably for a moment on some threshold—the entrance
to a church, office, or "public" building, or the point of access to
a "foreign" place—while passively, and usually "unconsciously,"
accepting a prohibition of some kind. Most such prohibitions
are invisible. Gates and railings, ditches and other material
barriers are merely the most extreme instances of this kind of
separation.

Henri Lefevbre, The Production of Space

With a single drop of ink for a mirror, the Egyptian sorcerer
undertakes to reveal to any chance comer far-reaching visions of
the past. This is what I undertake to do for you, reader. With this
drop of ink at the end of my pen I will show you the roomy workshop of Mr Jonathan Burge, carpenter and builder in the village of
Hayslope, as it appeared on the eighteenth of June, in the year of
our Lord 1799.

The afternoon sun was warm on the five workmen there, busy
upon doors and window-frames and wainscoting.

George Eliot, Adam Bede

If the opening of a novel may be imagined as a kind of threshold, the beginning of Eliot's *Adam Bede* resembles one perhaps more than most, because of the identity it establishes between our introduction to the novel and our introduction into the physical space of Adam's workshop. In that introduction, deference and command—or, to adopt Lefebvre's terms, invitation and prohibition—become indistinguishable from one another, as the suddenness with which we are thrust into the afternoon sun is framed as a favor or invitation: "what I undertake to do for you, reader." As in the Monty Python skit advising followers to "walk this way," the literal modeling of how we are to walk gives the lie to the presumption that we who are being guided are somehow in charge of the situation. For of course there is only one way to go, one way to "see" what we are figuratively being shown.

But what is the status of our figurative seeing, in the analogy between the threshold of the novel and that of physical space? A reader's tracing/ tracking of the printed word is matched by the revelations of the workshop, since the novel announces, after the words conveyed by Adam's "strong barytone" have been recorded on the page, that "such a voice could only have come" from the "broad chest" belonging to a "muscular man nearly six-feet high," just as it is "clear at a glance" that "the next workman is Adam's brother" (6). The clarity of the visual field is reinforced by the authority of the printed word, aligning the structure of the novel with Lefebvre's account of abstract space, in which, as he argues, our reliance on the written word reinforces the predominance of the visual in social space, and both are part of a modern (for Lefebvre, post-eighteenth century) translation of all sensory information into "the mere decipherment of messages by the eyes."[1] "Any non-optical impression—a tactile one, for example, or a muscular (rhythmic) one," he writes (as in Adam's singing), "is no longer anything more than a symbolic form of, or a transitional step towards, the visual" (286). Lefebvre calls the construction of space in this regime—a regime aligned with modern, production-oriented capitalist society—abstract space, and it shares its emphasis on visual display with the realist novel (287). Both offer a realm of images that in their apparent appropriateness and functionality give us no reason to look behind the curtain, or even to suspect that there is one: no reason to see in the description of

Adam's workshop, or in the beginning of a novel, anything other than a welcoming invitation.[2]

And yet, as Lefebvre argues, abstract space is political, its prescriptions and prohibitions and our orientation to them constituting the apparently given, seemingly unquestionable properties of the spaces we inhabit. Those spaces, like the structures represented in realist fiction, are not natural but hierarchical, ordered and organized into signs: sites for work and leisure; for family; for economics; for religion. Just as the drop of ink transmuted into the sorcerer's mirror allows us to "see," via a fantasmatic transmutation of words on the page into imagined vision, the roomy workshop of Mr. Jonathan Burge, so too does the ease with which we accept the invitation and, for that matter, the willingness with which we accept it as an invitation (rather than a prescription or prohibition) signal the naturalization of what Lefebvre has called the logic of visualization. Or, as he puts it more vehemently, "[S]igns have something lethal about them" (289). Imagination is a licensed trespasser, we are told elsewhere in *Adam Bede*, and not only does Eliot give us our provisional license, but she tells us precisely how to use it. "Put your face to one of the glass panes in the right-hand window: what do you see? . . . And what through the left . . . " (72). "The dairy was certainly worth looking at . . . such coolness, such purity, such fresh fragrance of new-pressed cheese, of firm butter. . . . But one gets only a confused notion of these details when they surround a distractingly pretty girl of seventeen . . . rounding her dimpled arm to lift a pound of butter out of the scale" (83). The novel's represented spaces, characters, and sometimes readers as well appear substantial, thing-like, embodied. But that very substantiality, Lefebvre's account of prohibition suggests, is an effect of the barrier between realist representation and its readers: a barrier that is often glass-like—invisible—but just as frequently visible, in the novel's insistence on the frame that surrounds the glass or the presence of frames such as doorways or windows, structures that literalize the threshold on which characters and readers are situated.[3]

This "look but don't touch" construction situates ordinary life as spectacle and readers as observers of a fixed display. Licensed as we are, our license is limited, our trespassing fully scripted, engineered so that what might have felt delightfully risqué—oh look, we are in Mr. Irwine's dining-room, or rather we are not really in it, but only peeking in—takes shape more as a directed tour, during which we are told exactly where we can look and what we will see, and indeed what we will think about what we see. "The walls, you see, are new and not yet painted . . . you suspect at once that the inhabitants of this room have inherited more blood than wealth" (54). "If you want to know more particularly how he looked, call to your remembrance some tawny-whiskered, brown-locked, clear-complexioned young Englishman whom you have met with in a foreign town . . . I will not be so much of a tailor as to trouble your imagination with the difference of costume, and insist on the striped waistcoat, long-tailed coat, and low-top boots" (61). Perhaps never has the phrase "you see" felt so peremptory, as readers are instructed to use their imaginations only to call a well-defined image to mind, the narrative keeping them so tethered to its represented space that it in fact sometimes imagines them into that space alongside the narrator, as if to make sure they do not use their license to stray too far: "Let me take you into that dining-room, and show you the Rev. Adolphus Irwine. . . . We will enter very softly, and stand still in the open doorway" (54). To borrow Garrett Stewart's phrase, perhaps never has there been a more conscripted reader than the reader of *Adam Bede*.[4]

It is not surprising that the realist novel tethers us to what it wants us to see, the precision with which we are placed—left window or right—a matter of supporting the novel's realism by situating readers precisely within its represented space. What stands out in *Adam Bede* are the shortness of our leash and the explicitness of our duties—the numerous cautions and limitations suggested by the term "trespassing." But the insistence with which our path is charted is in fact crucial to this novel's construction of what at least one definition of ideology (Althusser's) conceives of, in spatial terms, as an imaginary relation to the real. Inviting us to imagine and at the same time telling us what the content of our imaginings will be, *Adam Bede* emphasizes this relation in a manner many realist novels perform more quietly, and in doing so exposes what is at stake for realist fiction in readers' acceptance of such directions. For this novel's particularity in delineating its spaces and structures and marking its readers' spatial and subjective orientation toward them encourages us to accept, and demonstrates our acceptance of, the obligatory relations and ideological orientations (toward work, family, gender, nation) that Lefebvre groups under the category of prohibition. Disciplining the direction of desire so that fancy or imagination—what might fill the space of a novel—is both anticipated and pre-empted by what the novel defines as the real (so that realism's characteristic illusions arrive, effectively, pre-disillusioned), the novel reveals in our dutiful following of its directions the acceptance of a proscribed, pre-seen landscape that constitutes what I want to call its realist fantasy. *Adam Bede*'s construction of space—especially its construction of home and its situating of readers in relation to Victorian domesticity—articulates and overlaps with the ideological prescriptions and prohibitions the inhabiting of that space entails. Locating readers at thresholds that are conceived of as both literal and figurative—thresholds that tie the invitation to enter to a prohibition against doing so—the novel renders the real desirable by keeping the reader on the outside looking in, and by rendering its contents as palpable objects and experiences whose visceral nature (touch, sounds, and scents) are constructed as participatory experiences. The "real" is thus rendered simultaneously as accessible and as always slightly out of reach.

These invitations and prohibitions build the novel's realism. Theorists have argued that classic realism represses the signs of its own production: that realist prose, with its illusion of transparency, affects merely to communicate.[5] And yet as in the analogy between the reading of words on a page and the reading of spatial signs or cues, realism in this sense is not just a reinforcing of dominant values but a rebuilding of them: every realist novel has to construct its realism from the ground up. Realism, like the real, or, as in a useful formulation by Deleuze and Guattari, like home, "does not pre-exist. Rather, it is necessary to draw a circle around that uncertain and fragile center, to organize a limited space."[6] Realist representation takes as given the structures it puts in place (hence the term "description" plays right into its hand), and its descriptions are also prescriptions, a circle drawn around a specified center, the organization of a limited space. Like the process of Althusserian interpellation, realist representation performs itself over and over again. And not only does it build the illusion of a certain kind of space, but it is said (most prominently by Ermarth) to

construct and depend on consensus.[7] Realist space—space as it is constructed in the realist novel—must represent what "everyone" agrees
constitutes the real, and yet this consensus is confined to a limited and
proscribed circle: its imagined readers.

Like home, then, realism is in the business of cordoning off as well as
inviting in, producing in a single structure what Lefebvre has called the
space of "no" and the space of "yes": the prescriptive forms that define
social space.[8] And because subjectivity tends to be imagined in relation
to a particular imagining of space—because the nineteenth century in
particular, with its emphasis on interiority, imagined authentic subjects
as inhabiting a certain kind of space—the question of realist space is
simultaneously epistemological and social, literal and metaphorical,
relying on connections the period made between specific formations
of identity and the space in which one might find them. Realism's
emphatic concern with readers' and characters' relations to represented
space invites us to examine the mediations and prohibitions of the novel's world, and indeed of the world of which it is a part as well. And in
exchange for our acceptance of its mediations and prohibitions, both of
these—the world of the novel, and the world of public and private spaces
the novel seeks to represent—offer what have long been understood as
the particular pleasures of realist reading, including the coherence of
social space and of the reader's identity as that identity is situated within
and structured by it.

"All property can be defined in terms of a kind of mirror effect," writes
Lefebvre (186). "On the one hand, one . . . relates oneself in space, situates oneself in space . . . . One places oneself at the center, designates
oneself, measures oneself and uses oneself as a measure. One is, in short,
a subject" (182). "[A]s mirror and mirage," he continues, landscape
"presents any susceptible viewer with an image at once true and false of
a creative capacity which the subject (or Ego) is able, during a moment
of marvelous self-deception, to claim as his own" (189).

Here is Anthony Trollope, in his autobiography, commenting on
one of the marvelous self-deceptions by means of which he constituted
himself as a subject and an author.

> I have explained, when speaking of my school days, how it came
> to pass that other boys would not play with me. . . . Study was not
> my bent, and I could not please myself by being idle. Thus it came
> to pass that I was always going about with some castle in the air
> firmly built within my mind. For weeks, for months . . . I would
> carry on the same tale. . . . I myself was my own hero. In after years
> I have done the same,—with this difference, that I have discarded
> the hero of my early dreams, and have been able to lay my own
> identity aside. (43)

Trollope's account of how he came to write realist novels begins with
the story of his father's failed attempts at two projects, authorship and
fatherhood—both marked by an inability to raise his family out of poverty, or, to make explicit the connection as the son does not quite do,
the failure of his literary endeavors (what the son describes as a singu-
larly uninteresting and laborious ecclesiastical dictionary) to put a solid
roof over the family's heads. Indeed, what Trollope calls the "futile pile
of literature" that was his father's life's work is both metaphorically and
metonymically tied to the pile in which the family lived: a badly sag-
ging farmhouse "which always seemed to be in danger of falling into the
neighbouring horsepond" (11).

Trollope's autobiography showcases the difference between the
father's attitude and achievements and the son's, detailing the way in
which the publication of novels allowed the latter to rise far above the
mud and muck of his childhood, fulfilling the fairy-tale promise of the
"castles" he made up for his own enjoyment: "This," he writes of his adult
life, "has been so exactly the life which my thoughts and aspirations had
marked out" (168). And yet despite the fulfillment of his own childhood fantasy in becoming the famous Anthony Trollope, it is not just
the publication of the novels, but indeed their very conception—their
realism—that this text constructs both in opposition to and in contrast
with his father's failures. The transformation of the castle-in-the-air,
itself defiantly set "firmly in my mind," into the more homely structure
of the realist novel (and, somewhat ambiguously, the removal of himself
as hero—as if it is understood that no other candidate will emerge to fill
the position) is itself a rejection of the insubstantial and fantastical—the

raw "castle" material for the solidly real. Trollope represents the development of his career as a transformation of the insubstantial into the substantial; of failure into success; of the "futile pile of literature" into a solid, income-producing list of titles made up of recognizably realist characters: novels whose utility and practical value are notoriously ratified by the sales figures listed alongside them at the autobiography's end.

Indeed, the *Autobiography* proudly reproduces a description of Trollope's work that attests to the way in which, in Trollope's fiction, the object of representation has been fully domesticated, its fantasy-aspect shifted from content to relationship, the ordinariness of the object transformed by the reader's exclusion from it. Trollope's novels are "just as real," writes Nathaniel Hawthorne, "as if some giant had hewn a great lump out of the earth and put it under a glass case, with all its inhabitants going about their daily business, and not suspecting that they were being made a show of" (144). Reality and fantasy combine seamlessly in this image of ordinary people being watched by a giant: an image of a Lilliputian world so masterfully controlled that its inhabitants emphatically betray no evidence that they know they are being observed.

But the image Hawthorne conjures up is not in fact a Lilliputian one. The giant's presence defines a realistic scale for life lived under the glass case: what is a toy world for a giant would be just the right size for us. The giant is realist omnipotence, hovering over what stands as a found object: a lump of earth displaying no signs of producer or production. And yet what he is also hovering over, in a kind of multiplication of images of Trollope himself, is an image of the author's mind as the autobiography describes it: a mind with a novel already in it, in the shape of a town and its emphatically oblivious inhabitants, going about their business, failing to suspect that they are "being made a show of."

This image of a mind enclosing a town and its inhabitants is not just an image of Trollope's mind, but a paradigmatic image of the Victorian realist novel as well. Representing the novel as a chunk of ordinary life, it projects what I want to call a fantasy of solidity: an ordinary world sequestered as if it were an interior world, an outside that is also an inside. "What didn't the nineteenth century invent some sort of casing for!" asked Walter Benjamin; the answer, of course, is nothing.[9] In Trollope's and Hawthorne's paradigmatic images of realism, and in Eliot's exemplary realist novel as well, realism's apparent solidity serves as its "real" estate, constructing and feeding readerly fantasies about a world of ordinary people "going about their daily business, and not suspecting that they were being made a show of." Moreover, situating readers at the metaphorical threshold of a house or home or window, this image situates them (us) at an ontological threshold as well. For what kind of fantasy, exactly, is a fantasy of solidity, of ordinary people going about their business? The realist novel comes into being, in this scenario, as a paradoxical construction in which the solid, thing-laden world of the Victorians is exactly what is wanted: it is an inside made into an outside, an outside that represents an inside; a fantasy that vehemently denies its status as one.

"Daily business," as in Hawthorne's image of Trollope's realism, is what the realist novel according to this definition reflects and reproduces; "daily business" proceeds without interruption, oblivious to everything except itself, and perhaps especially oblivious to the panoptic machinery that makes it go. For realism's best subject is the one whose demeanor announces that he or she is nobody's creation: that he or she has certainly not been produced as an object of entertainment. What could possibly be entertaining about people going about their ordinary business? And yet Hawthorne's glass cover somewhat counterintuitively figures this banal world as a world on display, that exists to be seen—a world in which we might, for instance, come across something like this:

[T]he broad chest belonged to a large-boned muscular man nearly six feet high, with a back so flat and a head so well poised that when he drew himself up to take a more distant survey of his work, he had the air of a soldier standing at ease. The sleeve rolled up above the elbow showed an arm that was likely to win the prize for feats of strength; yet the long supple hand, with its broad finger-tips, looked ready for works of skill. In his tall stalwartness Adam Bede was a Saxon ... but the jet-black hair ... and the keen glance of the dark eyes that shone from under strongly marked, prominent, and mobile eyebrows, indicated a mixture of Celtic blood. (6)

As numerous critics have noted, the ideological investments of this passage could hardly be clearer, the image itself more idealized, less "realistic." Eliot's staging of Adam as spectacle epitomizes the idea of realism as a fantasy of solidity, one metonymically reinforced by his status as a maker of reliably solid objects as well as by his absorption in his task, an attention that seals him "inside" the text even as his exemplary status refers his meaning elsewhere, to some putative observer. A maker of frames, his admire-but-don't-touch physique is framed as well by the numerous contexts in which the narrator situates it as well as by that narrator's admiring eye, inscribed in the spectacularized surface of his body itself, with its arm that shows, its hand that looks, its eyes that shine. Though Hetty Sorrel bears the burden of critical opprobrium in this novel for her overt solicitation of the male gaze, the entire text of *Adam Bede* is an incitement to vision, shaped by a narrator who acts as tour guide and by the ideological screens or frames that, like Hawthorne's glass case and like the narrator in this valuation of Adam, tell readers how to "see" the objects they enclose.

In its ambiguous status as a show-that-is-not-a-show, a performance of everyday life, such images of an enclosed but outwardly-oriented body reinforce the doubleness of the modern subject whose everyday life is lost to representation (as Michael Fried has argued) because the conditions of its visibility are inscribed within it.[10] In *Adam Bede*, the presence of images and structures that enclose and define the real, especially structures (like those Adam himself builds) associated with the home—doorways, windows, and frames—signal the enclosedness and interiority of the space they delimit even as they open it to scrutiny. *Adam Bede*'s realism reproduces a cultural imaginary in which the reader, imagined as viewer or spectator, stands at the threshold of—and is invited to imagine entering—a space constructed as simultaneously real and fantasmatic: in Lefebvre's terms, a space of no that is also a space of yes.

Eliot encloses her narrative within the framework of the narrator's cognition and bodily presence; she situates herself at the threshold between reader and text and between invisibility and embodiment. Calling herself, briefly, an old friend of Adam Bede's, she even seems to occupy a doubly gendered space.[11] She encloses the narrative as well in the historical past while opening it to the present as she invites readers to participate as contemporaries, becoming the kind of pedestrians she praises in her review of Riehl, on which this novel draws for its realist ideals.[12] Her touristic direction reproduces the distancing mechanisms on which Victorian realist fiction often drew, while its representations of private space—our glimpses of Adam's workshop, Mrs.Poyser's kitchen, the bedrooms of Hetty and Dinah—valorize even as they violate bourgeois interiority. And in a manner that seems designed to amplify even as it frustrates an imagined fantasy of inclusion in the solid realist world, the narrator at several points evokes the reader's bodily presence, as in our introduction to the Hall Farm, in which she asks us as "licensed trespassers" to press our faces against the window (71). In all of these ways, this novel situates us, sometimes along with its narrator and characters, on a threshold, where we might, as Adam does at a significant moment, hesitate—our hesitation marking, as my epigraph from Lefevbre suggests, the unarticulated prohibitions that structure all these oppositions.

In one of Adam's moments of marvelous self-deception, he hears a bustling in the kitchen of his mother's house and descends the stairs, hopeful but also doubtful, there to find someone other than the person he wishes to see. The scene has a dreamlike quality to which the novel itself alludes, as Adam's imagination conjures up Hetty's image but reality offers him Dinah instead:

> Adam's imagination saw a dimpled face, with dark bright eyes and roguish smiles. . . . A very foolish thought—it could not be Hetty; but the only way of dismissing such nonsense from his head was to go and see *who* it was, for his fancy only got nearer and nearer to belief while he stood there listening. He loosed the plank, and went to the kitchen door.
>
> "How do you do, Adam Bede?" said Dinah. . . .
>
> It was like dreaming of the sunshine, and awaking in the moonlight. . . . [H]er slim figure, her plain black gown, and her pale serene face, impressed him with all the force that belongs to a reality contrasted with a preoccupying fancy. (116)

The only way to dismiss the nonsense from your head and get to the real, this passage instructs, is to cross the threshold. Adam's hesitation at this moment might be said to express his wish not to discover what, he suspects, he will discover—his intuition that he will not see what he wants to see, but rather what he ought to see—what the disciplinary narrator, explicitly disciplining his fancy by giving him reality (with all its force) instead, wants him to see. The scene has all the hallmarks of a prohibition disguised as an invitation: of a realism in which realism's supposed alternative, fantasy, is what I earlier called pre-disillusioned, accompanied by the suspicion that it *is* fantasy. Recapitulating the movement of the plot as a whole, this scene works to alter the trajectory of Adam's fancy, or to show that it has already been altered: to discipline his desire by substituting Dinah for Hetty. And indeed the result of his finding Dinah here, in his mother's house, is a dawning of interest in her (marked, as readers of the novel will recall, by her uncharacteristic blush).[13]

The scene follows the trajectory of much realist narrative, which teaches us to expect that our illusions will not be fulfilled; which tries to teach us—or teaches us to try—to prefer our disillusionments. Staging the difference between the two women as a function of Adam's perception, this episode also suggests that they (the women) are exchangeable: placeholders for a specific function, stand-ins for one another, they participate in the interchangeability the novel requires, substantiating the exchange of what is called fantasy (the insubstantial, the unreliable) for what is defined as its opposite (solidity, reliability). As in another scene in which Hetty appears in a dress like Dinah's and in Dinah's own cap, startling those who see her with the unexpected juxtaposition of her face with Dinah's demure hood—the wrong picture in the frame—it is as if Eliot has switched the heads of each character to the other's body, in a weird game in which body parts are disassembled, disorienting readers, evoking an impulse we didn't know we had to reassemble them correctly. But if our corrective impulse kicks in, along with the narrator's (and along with Adam's, at the kitchen threshold) this is merely an indication of the well-trained realist readers we have become. For Adam's suspicion that it cannot be Hetty downstairs–the dawning awareness that his whimsy must turn out to be, in the novel's context, mere fantasy–signals the larger miscalculation of which everyone (readers included) but he is fully conscious, and is but a single small step in a series of necessary and increasingly painful corrections, during the course of which he comes to see what he is meant to see and to desire what he is meant to desire, as dictated by the prescriptions of this novel's spaces and invitations.

Adam's problem is not just a case of not getting what you wish for or of wishing for the wrong thing, but rather of misreading the relation between the frame and its contents. Hetty does not fit the mother's house, just as her face is not suited to Dinah's cap; this is not her context; this is not a scene in which she would appear. Adam's reading of the space, like his reading of Hetty, is exposed as a misreading, a moment at which, as he rightly suspects, his fancy has produced the wrong image, and the home itself, as if self-correcting, produces the right one. His job, like ours, is to see what he is supposed to see, what the space of which he is a part prescribes that he see, and more precisely to recognize the figure that belongs to the space, as we are told to do with our mental image of someone "like" Arthur Donnithorne: to project into the designated space of our own minds as well as of Arthur's parlor its proper occupant. That Hetty's face does not "fit" Dinah's cap; that this can't be Hetty in his mother's house; that Adam does not realize what the scene realizes for him—such moments are not just examples of the novel's corrections of vision but also instances of the novel's construction of its realist fantasy, specifically of Hetty's eventual physical displacement, necessitated by her inability to belong to the novel's social space. Blurring the difference between the space of no and the space of yes (walk *this* way), the novel employs a strategy of substitution dedicated to promoting the attractiveness of the real, which turns out to hinge on a solidity associated with vision itself. The substantiality of what is present is pitted against the insubstantiality, the unlikeliness, and indeed the inappropriateness of what, in the context of Adam's dream, is termed his "preoccupying" fancy: the illusion wrongly occupying the space where reality should be. Offering a salutary real in place of a misleading fancy, the scene records the disciplining of a trespassing vision, the redirecting of a gaze that had wanted to go elsewhere.

But the novel makes this kind of mistake easy: anyone could be Adam, imagining what he imagines, since what the novel insists upon is less the person than the structure, less the figure than the figure in a certain space—a woman in a frame. In fact, *Adam Bede* includes a number of images of framed women, most notably in the "Two Bedchambers" chapter, in which Dinah looking out of her window is contrasted with Hetty gazing into her mirror. Among these are several images of a woman in a doorway. Sometimes that character is Adam's mother, waiting for him to come home, as she does near the novel's beginning; sometimes it is Mrs. Poyser; the novel in fact begins and ends with such an image. Situating women at the thresholds of houses, Eliot locates them at what, Beatriz Colomina points out, is that structure's most vulnerable point: the point that creates an opposition between inside and outside; the point at which, as Lefebvre notes, one might unconsciously hesitate; the point that signals both invitation and exclusion.[14] And the opposition and necessary exchange between inside and outside, interior and exterior, interiority and exteriority that the threshold marks is both allegorized and epitomized, in this novel, in the opposition between, as well as necessary exchange of, Dinah and Hetty.

When *Adam Bede* suggests, as it does in the kitchen scene and at other points as well, the exchangeability of Hetty and Dinah (as in the appearance of Hetty in Dinah's clothing, or the presence of both names in Hetty's pocket-book—"she will not say which is her own name," reports Mr. Irwine, after Hetty's arrest for the murder of her child [408]), what is it, one might well ask, that could be exchanged? The two characters are, after all, so different. Here is Dinah:

> Everything was looking at its brightest at this moment, for the sun shone right on the pewter dishes, and from their reflecting surfaces pleasant jets of light were thrown on mellow oak and bright brass;— and on a still pleasanter object than these; for some of the rays fell on Dinah's finely-moulded cheek, and lit up her pale red hair to auburn, as she bent over the heavy household linen which she was mending for her aunt. No scene could have been more peaceful. (73–74)

This is a picture of domestic realism; indeed, it is a painting of domestic realism, a scene out of Dutch painting, notably Dutch painting of the seventeenth century. The woman peeling carrots in Eliot's discussion of Dutch realism in *Adam Bede*'s seventeenth chapter (another framed woman) is usually read as a metonym for the "humble realism" said to characterize *Adam Bede* itself.[15] But Dutch painting as Eliot uses it here may be understood to refer not only to the mundane material realities with which it is usually associated and with which the narrator herself associates it, but also to those images of enclosure, privacy, and seclusion associated with bourgeois realism in the nineteenth century: an idea of interiority that several critics, among them John Lukacs, describe as the bourgeoisie's most notable contribution to Western culture. This interiority, Lukacs argues, is best exemplified by "a Dutch or French master, of the seventeenth or of the late nineteenth centuries . . . a Vermeer or a Rembrandt, a Monet, a Pissaro, or a Sisley—very different painters who, nevertheless, have one thing in common. Their works exemplify the rich interior lives of our ancestors. By this I do not merely mean their subjects, the rooms painted by Vermeer," writes Lukacs; "What unites them is their preoccupation with illumination, the attempt of their genius to paint not so much what exists around us as what is visible to us. . . . Their enlightenment is of an interior, not an exterior, nature."[16]

Lukacs describes here a bourgeois fantasy of privacy, comfort, and security, signified by the representation of an architectural interior that is also a rendering of subjectivity. Scenes such as these, which reflect an increasing interest in the enclosed spaces of private life, articulate, by way of images of absorption, security, and comfort, and especially the quality of a certain kind of light, a certain kind of interior landscape: a landscape of the mind. And as such scenes construct bourgeois subjectivity, they also build the external, solid space in which it lives: "The interior furniture of houses appeared together with the interior furniture of minds" (623). The room in which Dinah sits mending linen, that is, is a stage set for the construction and presentation of bourgeois subjectivity, an image that collapses subjectivity and interiority and makes the latter—and not just its light, but its particular kind of interior space, with its particular kind of furniture, and the particular things one would tend to find there (pewter, brass, linen), along with a demonstration of the kind of absorbed attention they require (polishing, sewing) into a condition for the production of the former. Focused on her task in such a way as to require the presence of a beholder (like Adam at the novel's beginning), Dinah forms a picture of absorption that solicits the viewer's gaze, the scene constructing its domesticity as if behind glass. Thus as the plates redirect the sunlight so that household objects reflect beams from Dinah's cheek and hair, the reflected light forms a closed circle, a visible rendering of interiority, captured in both interior and external projections of specific values: realism as fantasy, in the form of a selection and arrangement of people and things.[17]

What a self not identified with such a place and such values might look like is an image the novel provides as well. To see what exteriority looks like, we can turn to Hetty Sorrel, whose presence in the communal and domestic spaces of Eliot's novel is marked by her self-exclusion from them: an exclusion signaled (as opposed to Dinah's attention to any domestic need) by her inattentiveness to her surroundings, the state of distractedness which finds her never intent upon her work, but rather using its gestures to show off her pretty arms; a state in which she is always dreamily seeing herself elsewhere.[18] Hetty's punishment literalizes her displaced and absent sensibility. "She had quite lost her way in the fields, and might as well go in one direction as another, for aught she knew" (385). "How she yearned," we are told, when she finds herself in a stranger's house, at the end of her resources, contemplating her narrow possibilities, "to be back in her safe home again, cherished and cared for as she had always been!" Quick to correct as always, the narrative continues, "Her aunt's scolding about trifles would have been as music to her ears right now" (379). "Now for the first time," the narrative reads, "she felt that her home had been a happy one, that her uncle had been very good to her"; that it "was what she would like to wake up to as a reality, and find that all the feverish life she had known besides was a short nightmare" (371). The novel offers its most extended interior monologue on behalf of a character who has failed, until this point, to understand the necessity and indeed the pleasures of the prohibitions under which she labored; a character in whom, perhaps because of this, it has not yet been possible to detect the presence of any interiority worth noting. And it offers this monologue, moreover, as an extended reflection on an experience of enforced exteriority (we might call it an exterior monologue): the representation of a state of misery that results from and is identified with wandering, accompanied by a new awareness of exclusion from that "safe home" whose admonitory pleasures the wanderer had not previously appreciated. If readers have found it difficult to accept as belonging to Hetty the interiority Eliot seems to represent in the scene of Hetty by the dark pool contemplating suicide because the novel has not granted her a similar consciousness elsewhere, it is perhaps because of the generalizeable contrast which is the scene's disciplinary point: the contrast between the sense of place, or orientation, offered by the boundaries and prescriptions of home (now explicitly marked as the space of yes, or social space) on the one hand, and the absence of markers, the inability to orient the self, in the context of nature (defined as the space of no—the space that is not social and allows such things as child-murder to take place) on the other. From the perspective of "Poor Hetty," who never knew it before, prohibition equals comfort; the space of no (where one was scolded) is in fact the space of yes.[19]

Adam Bede shows us, as readers, a series of pictures: the picture of Hetty's wanderings, certainly, but more often the kind of Dutch painting in which we find Dinah. And, as in the request that we imagine someone like Arthur, it asks for our collaboration in constructing these images. Furnishing our minds even as she refers us to the furnishings we are supposed to hold therein to help us appropriately furnish her novel, Eliot both projects the social space that houses our subjectivities and invites us to construct it for ourselves. Introduced into Adam's workshop, we note textures, scents, the quality of the light. We are directed toward evaluation, comparative coloring: Seth's hair is not as thick as Adam's; Mr. Irwine's wallpaper is not quite what it should be. Looking into Mr. Irwine's dining room, we read the condition of its inhabitants in the condition of their walls; we are taught how to understand what we see before we see it: "It is very pleasant," we are advised, "to have some men turn round" (56). We are referred, for descriptions of characters, to the comfort of our own recollections ("If you want to know more particularly how he looked, call to your remembrance ..." [61]). Bringing the full force of the imperative to conversation's casual "you see"—rendering explicit the realist directive that both invites and commands—the narration does not so much show us as tell us that we have in essence already seen whatever it has to display. *Adam Bede* is a novel in which imagination itself, perhaps in the form of any fantasies we might call our own—has been outlawed, and any attempt to imagine, even "your own" version of Arthur Donnithorne, has already been anticipated and corrected by the ever-vigilant narrator. But as we construct Arthur Donnithorne by consulting our memories of someone like him—"some tawny-whiskered, brown-locked, clear complexioned young Englishman whom you have met with in a foreign town" (61), we bring into being not only Arthur Donnithorne but ourselves as well: selves in whom the novel's prescriptive regime becomes indistinguishable from its realist fantasy, as it locates the real inside its readers' heads. Collapsing the distance between reader and representation, Eliot's narrator imagines reader and text as mutually constitutive, as in Elaine Scarry's account of the way we make objects in our own image: "human beings project their bodily powers and frailties into external objects . . . and then those objects in turn become the object of perceptions that are taken back into the interior of human consciousness . . . ."[20] If Scarry is right, what the novel calls into being here is not only the structure of realist fiction, which imbues in us an effect of the real by enlisting us in the realization of its contents, but the structure of our identities as well, since the objects we create "become the object of perceptions that are taken back into the interior" of our conceptions of ourselves. Being in on the subtle yet key distinctions that construct the novel's interiority (understanding the quality of the light that filters through Adam's workshop, as it does through Mrs. Poyser's kitchen; understanding why Hetty must be scolded, how it is that she fails to measure up) makes us co-producers and co-owners: this is our real estate as well.

Adam Bede thus enlists readers in the paradoxical construction of their own identities as effects of its strategies of representation. And yet in evoking not just the solidity of a realist landscape but that of the reader's body as well, it has the opposite effect—or rather, once again, a threshold effect, in which we are simultaneously included and excluded. For if any realist narrator's evocation of visual detail—that hallmark of realist narrative—bestows a vividness and solidity on the novel's represented world, the business of creating the reader through an explicit second-person address ("you see") might seem to amplify that effect, and its realism as well, by extending its offer of solidity to the reader. Like the hailing of Althusserian interpellation, which it echoes ("hey, you there"), the narrator reinforces the novel's fantasy of solidity by evoking the role of the body in the activity of seeing, producing our solidity as a means of substantiating its own.[21] And yet this very solidity is what keeps us, figuratively, outside: activating an image of readers' bodily materiality—the idea that readers just might intrude, physically, on the text—the prohibition of such imagined intrusion or trespassing must be mandated. The prohibition on entering functions as the sign of our material presence: it is what the novel offers in exchange for an acceptance of its strictures. And that same prohibition works metaphorically, as my discussion of the novel's opening suggested, to frame the novel itself as a house or home. The inseparability of the structures out of which the real is built from the fantasies they express is what I have been referring to as this novel's fantasy of solidity, and the hall of mirrors in which Eliot's conscripted reader is situated is the ordinary world in which we live. For even as the glass's transparency offers readers the "reality" of what lies behind it, even as we are invited to identify our own private Arthur Donnithornes, our involvement in the novel's reality effect depends on our exclusion: our presence on the threshold, our faces pressed against the glass.

I want to return to another moment of imagined exclusion, by way of Lefebvre's account of the repressive nature of social space as exemplified by an object held up for display and yet barred from use, by recalling that part of the novel in which Arthur visits Mr. Irwine but fails to confess what readers are told he intends to confess about his relationship with Hetty. The scene is an inviting one, full of seductively precise spatial and sensory detail. The narrator describes the richness of the room's interior light, the pleasures of the company it offers, the promise of a good breakfast: "the study lay on the left hand of this door, opposite the dining room. It was a small low room . . . yet it looked very cheery this morning as Arthur reached the open window. For the morning sun fell aslant on the great glass globe with gold fish in it, . . . and by the side of this breakfast-table was a group which would have made any room enticing" (168). As licensed trespassers (a term that takes as given the structure it puts in place), we are invited into this imagined space and just as emphatically barred from it, a tension reinforced by the fact that we know why Arthur is there and thus know what he fails, with tragic consequences, to say. Indeed, his inability to tell provokes and forecloses a readerly fantasy of interruption, his failure of nerve seeming to mirror, as it calls up, our own. What becomes a drama of enforced helplessness marks the novel as an example of Lefebvre's object on display: we can look but are not allowed to touch; we are allowed to breach a certain boundary, but only as trespassers; we can enter (as far as the threshold) provided we do not in fact intrude; we can be there, that is, provided we are not "really" there. The object offered up to the gaze and yet barred from any possible use is the realist novel, which in habituating us to its own prohibitions and assuming our habituation to them reveals the conscripted nature of its own and our realist territory.

And yet the scenario might also be said to imply an exchange, in which prohibition is the condition of both our knowledge and our presence. For what we receive in return for accepting the realist prohibition—for staying quietly on the threshold—is nothing other than ourselves, in the form of the novel's vivid evocations: of the sun on the glass bowl; the "two brown pups . . . in an ecstatic duet of worrying noises"; the "fragrant steam" emitted by the "silver coffee pot." Whether we imagine ourselves standing quietly in the doorway, feel the pressure of our faces on a window, or are so absorbed in the scene that we forget our trespassing bodies altogether, the materiality of this scene (transmitted as an effect of the visual) marks our indisputable presence. Reading and viewing, reading *as if* viewing, we enjoy both the "apparent reflective completeness" of realist representation as well as the shared meanings, the ability to comprehend the system of signs, that define the construction of social space.[22]

The novel ends as it began, with the image of a woman in a doorway looking out for Adam: "a figure we know well . . . shading her eyes with her hands as she looks for something in the distance" (537); ("The door of the house is open, and an elderly woman is looking out" [39]). The structure and language suggest, once again, that the character here is a placeholder: one of any number of women, readers included, who might fit or project themselves into this spot (Adam's identity is specified, while the woman's is not; even "the figure we know well" is not named in this paragraph). That this woman is a placeholder—a figure who might be replaced by any number of figures like her—also suggests the way in which the structure of the home replicates and reinforces the narrative's ideological frame, the reproduction of the image suggesting the reproduction of the family, on and on ad infinitum.[23] The exchangeability of Dinah and Hetty, along with the novel's other images of women in frames, suggest as well not just the possibility that the woman in the frame might be any woman, but also the status of any woman as both a figure on the threshold—a domestic angel who might "become" her fallen counterpart—and as a figure *for* that same threshold: for the difference, and mutually reinforcing nature of, the poles of outside and inside, exteriority and interiority. Bracketing the narrative between these two images as bookends or mutually reflecting mirrors, Eliot creates a structure in which the reader's flash of recognition, our feeling of having arrived at the right place—the realization that we have been here before (and that we are still, at the novel's end, on the threshold)—affirms both the novel's solidity and ours. And yet in referring, with this image, to ground it has itself established, the novel replaces the real with the imaginary in a manner that once again reproduces Althusser's definition of ideology. Bracketing or framing its own realism, *Adam Bede* reveals itself as an extended display or externalization of interiority, a closed system whose realism consists in showing us how it is that the imaginary replaces the real by framing itself doing so.

Chapter 2

How I Met Your Mother and other Lucky Accidents

1. *OLIVER TWIST* AND THE VICTORIAN FAMILY ROMANCE

In her essay "Nothing to Declare: Identity, Shame, and the Lower Middle Class," Rita Felski wonders about the tendency to understand class as a contingent aspect of identity. "For example," she writes, "if one has become upper-middle-class as a result of social mobility, then one really is upper-middle-class—class being, in one sense, nothing more than the sum of its material manifestations: the Anne Klein suits and goat-cheese souffles, the high-definition TV and the laptop computer, the postmodern novels and the holidays in Tuscany."[1] She goes on to question the assumption that we experience class as contingent or accidental, citing as an example Carolyn Steedman's *Landscape for a Good Woman,* a memoir that "portrays class identity as a structure of feeling, a complex psychological matrix acquired in childhood" (38). Steedman's description of the affective nature of class identity, and Felski's as well, bolstered by her own childhood recollections, validate the depth of the uneasiness displayed by, for instance, E. M. Forster's Leonard Bast, whose "laborious repartee and evident class insecurities mark him as a petit bourgeois aspirant towards a culture that can only be authentically inhabited by those who experience it from birth" (37). For Steedman and others, Felski posits, class identity is so deeply ingrained in affective or experiential identity—so profoundly a part of what we feel we are—that any alteration of it in later life, such as "rising" or "falling," evokes feelings of inauthenticity: of being something other than what one "really" is; of inhabiting an identity not one's own.

The tension between a notion of class identity as contingent and a sense that it is inherent appears in almost any Victorian novel one can think of, manifesting itself in a recurrent plot that, in its insistence on middle-class entitlement, has always seemed to protest too much, both in its structure and its persistence. This plot locates in the histories of its middle-class characters (and in the need to give them histories) a lineage presently unknown to them: a family located in the distant past, the discovery of which is accompanied by a modest but indisputably useful inheritance. This structure—long recognized as the mapping of a middle-class narrative onto an aristocratic one—articulates both the middle class's wish to distinguish itself from the aristocracy and its longing for some way to authenticate itself, erasing the contingent nature of class identity by claiming the ostensibly solid ground of ancestral connection.

But ancestral connection is not, I want to argue, what these plots most importantly discover. What they offer as a means of solving the problem of contingency, I wish to suggest, is love: or, more precisely, an affective narrative that not only shifts the business of lineage from the realm of property to that of feeling, but also transforms contingency into inevitability—or rather blends the two, reproducing what is perhaps the most significant aspect of aristocratic lineage for a middle-class person seeking to overcome a nagging sense of illegitimacy and instability. Writes Lawrence Stone of identity in the period preceding the rise of the nuclear family, "It was the relation of the individual to his lineage which provided a man of the upper classes in a traditional society with his identity, without which he was a mere atom floating in social space."[2] Replacing a lineage of blood with one of affect, the nineteenth-century novel anchors the floating self, accounting for the production of the meaningful subject (one who possesses "identity") in a manner that becomes central to, and indeed parallels, the realist novel's ability to invest the most ordinary circumstances—perhaps, the most apparently meaningless circumstances—with significance. The alignment of these seemingly contradictory claims—for accident or contingency, on the one hand, and necessity or inevitability on the other—constitutes the realist fantasy I wish to explore in this chapter.

In *Jane Eyre* and *Oliver Twist*, for example, the fantasy of being of noble birth, of having been born into the "wrong" family—or born into the right family but subsequently misplaced—tends to show the strain of its displacement to a middle-class context; the strain, that is, of trying to map a middle-class narrative onto an aristocratic one. A lineage of wealth is only partially replaced by one of character, aristocratic blood by family values (hence the need always to attempt to explain to one's students why it is that Jane, Oliver, and other characters end up inheriting money as well as family; why it is that family, character, and marriage, and above all, love—those things with which the aristocratic narrative of wealth is presumably being replaced—need to be supplemented with cash). What resists transmutation, in these narratives, is the sense that any contingency in the construction of identity must be erased: that there must be something fated or authentic about social status, and that a character who has to make his way to status rather than discovering that he was born into it—a character like Pip, in Dickens's *Great Expectations*; Henchard in Hardy's *Mayor of Casterbridge*; or Leonard Bast in *Howard's End*—will always be nagged by a sense of inauthenticity. Class identity in these novels is haunted by a fear of contingency, despite a general sense that the democratizing impulse to which it attests is an improvement over the fixed hierarchies of the past.

In the narrative Freud called the family romance, the child replaces his parents, in fantasy, with persons of higher social standing. In doing so, he "make[s] use . . . of any opportune coincidence from his actual experience, such as his becoming acquainted with the Lord of the Manor or some landed proprietor if he lives in the country, or with some member of the aristocracy if he lives in the town. Chance occurrences of this kind arouse the child's envy, which finds expression in a phantasy in which both his parents are replaced by others of better birth."[3]

Note the conflation of accident and inevitability here: this is the description of an accident that always happens. Freud's narrative (as Carolyn Steedman recounts it) is not so much a scene as a scenario: a psychodrama whose elements capture the symbolic structure of middle-class identity—that is, the accidental meeting need never take place in reality, for it always will in fantasy. And the imagining of an accident that always happens as a kind of primal scene of class identity links the idea of class identity's contingency with a sense of its inevitability, offering to the middle class a universal narrative of awakening to a "true" or deserved identity, while papering over the idea that not all members of the class of ordinary people will discover themselves to be noblemen or women in disguise.

Such meetings take a variety of forms in Victorian fiction. In *Great Expectations*, the childhood meeting between Pip and Estella evokes in Pip the feeling of shame and dissatisfaction that will shape his life, providing the groundwork for his expectations. In *The Mayor of Casterbridge*, the chance meeting between Henchard and Farfrae engenders in Henchard a feeling of inferiority, while Elizabeth-Jane possesses a nagging sense that she is never quite good enough, caused in part by her exposure to the higher-class affectations and aspirations of Lucetta, her potential stepmother. These examples alone suggest that, in realist fiction as in the class society it represents, the accident that prompts comparison is always bound to happen. Indeed, I wish to propose that the name for the inevitability that happens by accident, or the accident that always happens, is class identity. Included in the definition of class identity, that is, are two contradictory claims: it didn't have to be this way, and it could not have been any other way.

In these novelistic encounters, the inevitability of accident reinforces the mythic quality of social status. In particular, these meetings strengthen the tie between class identity and feeling: feeling in this narrative is already present but dormant. A novel may provide an objective correlative for it, as in Pip's early encounter with Magwitch: an event that serves as emotional ur-text both for his identity and for the structure of the entire novel. Emotion provoked by such moments is structured as a *mise-en-abyme*, as the accidental meeting awakens feelings more deeply grounded than any theoretical idea of class identity would suggest. And if the idea of the accidental meeting that provokes a journey to discover one's origins also seems accidental (it might just as easily not have happened), the idea that buried emotions are awakened by such a meeting suggests the opposite, positing feeling about class in these moments as an element of identity whose emergence is only a matter of time. And indeed, I want to suggest, Freud's accidental-meeting story, the family romance, appears in a number of Victorian novels in the form of another kind of romance, in which accident is more firmly tied to—is, indeed, transformed into—inevitability.

One of the strongest things that middle-class identity, as represented in Victorian fiction, has long had going for it—one element it has always been able to claim as a victory over the aristocratic way of doing things—is what Stone has dubbed "affective individualism": the shift from an ostensibly emotionally sterile, paternalistic structure of arranged marriages and deferential family bonds to a system in which marriage was founded on love, hierarchy replaced by the democratizing force of affection. As Stone writes, from the late sixteenth century to the eighteenth and nineteenth, family habits which encouraged deference and absolute paternal authority gave way to warmer human relationships and the development of what we call the nuclear family, including the concept that each person is unique (180). The idea of uniqueness, Stone suggests, would have increased the amount of affection family members lavished on one another, because each saw and respected the others as irreplaceable.

Whether one agrees with Stone or not, he seems here to pick up on a narrative promulgated most forcefully by the Victorian novel. Indeed, he structures this historical narrative, as the novels themselves do, as a trade-off: an exchange in which what a character or individual receives *instead of* aristocratic status is the uniqueness conferred by love and the affective family structure that comes with it. An absence of one kind of social status or specialness asserts itself as the presence of what has, in the construction of this exchange and in the context of middle-class ideology, become another. This is the realist fantasy I address in this chapter: the way these two novels—*Oliver Twist* and *The Mayor of Casterbridge*—both engage with and overturn the realist convention of the singularity or specialness of individual character. In Dickens's novel, this fantasy is both sustained and undermined by the idea of coincidence; in Hardy's, belief in individual uniqueness comes under pressure from the novel's exposure of the identity-effacing power of social institutions.

Dickens's *Oliver Twist* dramatizes such an exchange between aristocratic lineage and affective individualism. Oliver, born in the workhouse, is initially described as someone who "might have been the child of a nobleman or beggar" (3), evoking, of course, the structure of the family romance. His plot trajectory both duplicates the form of a discovery of aristocratic lineage and replaces that lineage with a network of affective ties: a replacement that asserts the superiority of affective relations over the "forced" and, in the novel's terms, unnatural connections determined by parents and property. Once Oliver's evil half-brother Monks and his schemes have been uncovered, the inheritance now known to be Oliver's can be restored to him, but his best inheritance, readers are meant to understand—the one that affirms the goodness he has unaccountably manifested all along—is his status as a "natural" child: the product of a loving bond between his parents Edward and Agnes. The most valuable part of his inheritance is the tracing of his origins to the relationship between his mother and his father: a story that stands in contrast, of course, to that of Monks, whose evil nature is, strangely enough but wholly in keeping with the novel's moralized biology, both biological and emotional, genealogically tied to the bad feeling that characterized his parents' marriage. But what I want to emphasize here, for the moment, is less the "how I met your mother" story (I will return to that) than the path that leads back to it: the way the narrative of accidental meetings by means of which Oliver's affective lineage is discovered reinforces, rather than undercutting, the idea of inevitability or stability, tying contingency to inevitability and using both to support the novel's realism.

A list of coincidences (assembled by Philip Horne) that take place in *Oliver Twist* reads as follows:

> The pocket picked by Charley and the Dodger when Oliver first goes out from Fagin's house happens to be that of Mr. Brownlow, the oldest friend of Oliver's father, and once in love with Oliver's aunt (now dead), who happens to have on his wall a portrait of Oliver's mother, which so resembles Oliver Mr. Brownlow is awestruck. When Sikes takes Oliver after his recapture to commit his second crime, at Chertsey, hours away from London, it turns out to be the house where Oliver's other aunt, Rose Maylie, lives. Oliver's father's will, destroyed by the father's wife, happens to have stipulated that Oliver inherits only if 'in his minority he

should never have stained his name with any public act of dishon-our, meanness, cowardice or wrong'—such a stain is just what fall-ing into Fagin's hands puts Oliver at risk of; Oliver's legitimate but wicked brother Edward Leeford ('Monks') happens to be the only one to know of this will, and to see and recognize Oliver, whom he has never seen (this time by his uncanny resemblance to their common father), on the one occasion he is away from Fagin's) and rescued by Mr. Brownlow. Somehow Monks connects with, and somehow finds, Fagin, whom he employs to recapture and criminalize him.

"All this contrivance is amazing," Horne concludes.[4]

Barry McCrea cites these events (and I follow him in using Horne's account) as evidence for what he sees as *Oliver Twist*'s failed realism; for McCrea, this series of coincidences affirms the extent to which "the abstract idea of genealogy is always working in opposition to" the nov-el's realism. "What," he asks, "are such contrivances doing in a novel so seriously and passionately concerned with painting a realistic portrait of society?"[5] But the narrative of the lucky accident (one way of describing the events Horne lists) validates a particular ideology of middle-class mobility, obscuring the fact that such a train of events or series of lucky accidents can hardly happen to everyone. Leaving aside for the moment the question of whether all the details Horne cites should be called coincidences, the abundance of accidental meetings and recognitions in *Oliver Twist* arguably has less to do with the problematic nature of the novel's realism (not itself, I would suggest in contrast to McCrea, a given) or the pull of the ancestral plot, than with the wholly realist idea (an idea, that is, compatible with realist ideology in the novel and in ordi-nary life) that someone who looks like a nobody might just "turn out to be" (in the language of coincidence used by Horne) fortunate and indeed special. Unrealistic as it seems, that is, coincidence is in fact a fantasy that validates the idea of the individual self's uniqueness, a validation on which capitalist society and realist narrative, and the construction of the realist subject as an effect of both, depend. As mathematician John Allen Paulos points out, "In reality, the most astonishingly incredible coinci-dence imaginable would be the complete absence of all coincidence.

Believing in the significance of oddities is self-aggrandizing," he adds. "It says, 'Look how important I am.' People find it dispiriting to hear, 'It just happened, and it doesn't mean anything.' "[6]

It is crucial that the noticing in Freud's family romance goes only one way: the Lord of the Manor or "member of the aristocracy" the child encounters is visibly identifiable as such, while the child who does the noticing is invisible, a version of the ordinary, middle-class individual, by definition not much to look at or remember. Such a chance encounter, in Freud's account, will inevitably arouse the envy of the lower-status child because, the story assumes, class envy is inevitable: dissatisfaction with one's own state will be awakened in the nobody by the apprehension of the somebody he will someday inevitably encounter. That Oliver is said to resemble both his mother and his father closely enough for this resemblance to be recognized by people in the street, or that he resembles his mother closely enough for Brownlow to be awestruck by the similarity, could, however, be taken to suggest not that the resemblance exists, but rather that it doesn't.[7] The exact points of resemblance between Oliver's mother's appearance and his own are never specified, and indeed could not be, without making Oliver into a less ordinary, more distinctive character than the novel's ideological purposes— requiring the ability of any ordinary reader to identify with Oliver— would support.[8] Cruikshank's illustrations represent Oliver as looking either like no one in particular or like anyone: his features are bland and indistinct, his face displaying an absence of minor-character eccentricity, suggesting both the moral purity that defines his character and a certain generic configuration of gender and class. The point for middle-class ideology might be that even the non-distinctive, the non-special, the people who look "like" everyone else (that is, the nobodies) are special for someone, and what makes them special and indeed recognizable, despite their nondescriptness, is the fact that they hold a position within a structure of affective relations.[9]

Oliver is rescued not by family but by friends, it might be argued, and most importantly restored not to blood relatives but to members of a loose network of those who love him, with affective ties replacing family relations. In fact the "family" in which he is finally ensconced includes both. Oliver's narrative effectively links blood and affection, subordinating the former to the latter to allow for a reconstruction of family along the lines of wish-fulfillment while linking it to genealogy and blood ties, replacing the idea of a rigid, pre-determined structure formed in the past with a more flexible arrangement that points simultaneously toward the blood and property ties of the past and the affective ties of the future. And in the narrative of Oliver's recognition and restoration to his family, familial (blood) relations and affective (friendship) relations are inextricably mixed via Brownlow, whose "how I met your mother" narrative—more precisely, "how I met your father" narrative—his part of the novel turns out in fact to be.

Subtly but effectively, Brownlow's narrative melds affective ties and familial ones, using the character of the former to adjudicate the nature of the latter. The story of Monks links coerced marriage (marriage for connections) to bad character: Monks is the "sole and most unnatural issue" of a marriage his father was "forced" and "ordered," because of "family pride," to make (396–97). Oliver's lineage, on the other hand, is the result of the intertwining of affective relations between his parents, his father, Edward Leeford, and Brownlow, Leeford's best friend— a connection established through the father's only sister, Brownlow's chosen wife, who died before they could be married. Oliver's father, described by Brownlow as possessing his sister's "soul and person" (397), attracts the attention and love of Agnes's father and of Agnes herself—the daughter's love represented, in Brownlow's narrative, as the inevitable reproduction of the father's. Ties between men and men and between men and women in this account are inseparable from, and indeed wholly entangled with, one another; love between men and women follows and duplicates, with the difference of sex, affection between men, while the opposite happens as well, as Brownlow's love for Oliver's father is described as following upon his love for the father's sister. This tangled tale of connections links family, marriage, and friendship until they are almost impossible to distinguish, one following another in a pattern of imitation and reproduction in which the production of children (Oliver and Monks) becomes the fulfillment of an emotional legacy which is also an endorsement of affective individualism over forced or arranged marriage. In this context, Oliver's illegitimacy becomes not a problem but rather an affirmation of affective individualism: his parents produced him out of the force of their feeling for one another, or what Brownlow melodramatically calls their "guilty and most miserable love" (415).

Brownlow, it turns out, knows what Oliver's mother looks like only from the portrait given to him (and painted by) his friend Leeford; he knows her as a picture, or portrait done in his friend's hand, an image mediated by his friend's perception. And when he comes upon Oliver, he recounts, "his strong resemblance to this picture I have spoken of, struck me with astonishment. Even when I first saw him in all his dirt and misery, there was a lingering expression in his face that came upon me like a glimpse of some old friend flashing on one in a vivid dream" (413). It is Leeford, not Agnes, that the picture recalls, or rather it recalls both of them; the image of the friend who painted the picture and passed it on to him is the image "in" Oliver's face, mediated by the picture he is also said to resemble. Brownlow is able to perceive Oliver's likeness to the portrait because of his own affective tie to Edward Leeford; Oliver, according to this logic, looks like his mother because of the affection that ties all these characters together. Both, that is, possess an expression that is not an effect of lineage alone, but of lineage backed by or combined with friendship. Oliver's resemblance to his mother is an effect of the chain of affective bonds in which Brownlow's narrative positions him. And the novel's end constructs for Brownlow—indeed, it is Brownlow's narrative that does the constructing—the family he was never able to have on his own: the family he might have had if his marriage to Leeford's sister had taken place. It makes Brownlow's "vivid dream" (413) a reality.

In his account of the rise of the affective nuclear family, Stone seeks to be dispassionate, cautioning his readers not to assume that there is anything morally reprehensible in the idea of marrying for economic reasons. But his discussion is inevitably informed by the rhetoric of the winning side, which is also that of the realist novel: by affective individualism itself, with its privileging of individual identity and choice. When he writes, for instance, that in the late sixteenth century parents began to "recognize that each child, even if it lived only for a few hours or days, had its own unique individuality" (257), the language of recognition places his account squarely in the tradition of the realist novel, which depends on recognition to support its ideas of uniqueness and individuality—terms Stone uses frequently—and to consolidate its effects. For recognition depends on the doubled narrative often characteristic of novelistic realism, in which a narrator knows the truth but refrains from revealing it until the novel's end. At that moment, when readers and characters come to possess knowledge the narrator already possesses, their joint awareness creates realist fiction's characteristic, retroactive coherence: the clearing up of all mysteries, the setting right of all difficulties, the apparent possession of or access to the real in light of present knowledge. And the value that is affirmed by the affective structure of the new nuclear family is similarly circular, created by the structure itself: since the family affirms the uniqueness of its members simply because they are included within it, the only requirement for "uniqueness" in the modern family is showing up.

The story of the chance encounter in Victorian fiction is, more often than not, as in Freud's family romance, a story about class. And yet that story, as if too disturbingly contingent, tends to be displaced onto a narrative in which contingency leads to an inevitability that eventually swallows it up: the story of how I met your mother tends to become a narrative about the inevitability of the subject produced by this affective union: about, in other words, you. The transformation of contingency into inevitability that structures what, stealing from the world of the situation comedy, I want to call the "how I met your mother" narrative reproduces the story of individual exceptionalism even as it democratizes it.[10] Within the terms of this narrative, romantic love is that mysterious something that renders class irrelevant—that, in the absence of aristocratic entitlement, transforms accident into inevitability—creating a logic that gives rise to a singular individual, a logic to which that individual can cling for a sense of authenticity. For the love story of one's parents, I wish to argue, is the narrative of accidental meeting whose contingency is erased by the existence of the subject produced by it. The narrative's destination, that is—the subject in whom it ends—could be anyone, and yet of course it never is: the recipient of this message, the one for whom it all makes sense, had, as the song says, to be you. In this sense at least, what McCrea wants realism to be—a series of random, unrelated events—is never the realism of the nineteenth-century novel, nor is it the realism of the universe most of us, as realist subjects, inhabit. Despite Roland Barthes's assertion that realism's marker is the detail that fails to signify, Victorian realism, with its inevitable tying up of all contingencies into narrative coherence and the production of a coherent subject, profoundly fears such randomness—a randomness that would suggest, along with the replacement of known lineage by contingent class, the replacement of a determined, known identity by a floating, atomistic one. In this reading, what looks like the overdetermination of Oliver's identity in a series of unlikely coincidences signals not the absence of realism in the magical pull of genealogy, as McCrea would have it, but rather the presence of realism as informed by the requirements of its fantastically coherent subjects.

It has often been noted that Oliver is never the motivator of his own discovery; the passivity that afflicts him when it comes to participating in Sikes's burglary plan or possibly escaping from Fagin's den colors his relation to the discovery of his history, which in the novel is everyone's concern but his. His reconnection to his past is the result of work done chiefly by Mr. Brownlow, for instance, to confirm the inchoate feelings that gentleman has about Oliver: feelings based on his resemblance to the portrait, but also on an unexplained intuition of the boy's goodness, the worth discernible through his ragged clothes. Oliver himself fails to recognize those who recognize him, or to seek any special significance in the events that befall him; rather, the world works on his behalf, in effect providing or staging the "coincidences" that enable him to be recognized as the special boy he "turns out" to be. This failure to recognize, and indeed the absence of any felt need to recognize on Oliver's part, suggests that the subject of such a narrative need not be possessed of any special knowledge to have his specialness perceived. Moreover, this absence of knowledge or agency allows Oliver to escape the complexities of resentment and desire manifested by Dickens's later character, Pip, whose knowledge of his conflicted identity and obvious imperfections leads to his condition as ultimately unlovable and, depending upon one's reading of the novel's several endings, possibly unmarriageable as well. Oliver's innocence also preserves ours, as readers, averting our attention from the double-take, or double-talk, embedded in the phrase "how I met your mother," which puts into play without precisely articulating the Oedipal fantasy driving the story—the easy interchangeability of personal pronouns permitting, even inviting us to say, or to think before we correct ourselves, "how I met *my* mother." The slip is avoided, the correction made, by the setting of the narrative in the past, and the insistence that "you," the subject toward whom the narrative is directed, are not the younger version of the father but rather the child produced by a past union, a child whose knowledge of past events—of his own ancestral history—is necessarily missing. (There is, however, an interesting moment in which Oliver does "meet" his mother: he describes the portrait not as an image he recognizes, as he might recognize his own—as Brownlow's shock suggests—but rather as an admonitory gaze: "the eyes look so sorrowful; and where I sit, they seem fixed upon me. It makes my heart beat . . . as if it was alive, and wanted to speak to me, but couldn't" [90]. For all the discussions of "eyes" in this novel—the eyes that pursue Sykes, and that Fagin perceives everywhere in the scene of his last night alive, it is striking that few if any critics have noticed the eyes that follow Oliver, suggesting a mother's monitoring gaze, in this case from beyond the grave).[11]

Thus (finally) the significance, for this reading, of the situation comedy "How I Met Your Mother" (US; 2005–2014), which I want to appropriate chiefly for its title and its premise, since they recapitulate and indeed inspired some of the issues about the Victorian family I have engaged here. The show's conceit is that one of its players will turn out to be, in the imaginary future, the father of the imaginary child the series addresses—"your" father, to use its own terms—and that the perfect mate for whom the protagonist constantly searches will turn out to be "your" (projected as the viewer's) mother. The formulation "how I met your mother" thus participates in the transformation of contingency into inevitability I have described, positioning accident—"how I met"—alongside destiny: the inevitable appearance of the person already marked, significantly, not as "my" wife, but as "your" mother—you being the destination, the subject who makes all contingency disappear.

The "how I met" conceit is connected to the novelistic structures I have been discussing in other ways as well, including:

1. The unabashed, explicit interpellation of the viewer. Whoever you are, it's *your* mother we're talking about.

2. The way the show was constructed so as to give the lie, weekly, to its title; you (the addressee), it seemed to tell us, will *never* know how I met your mother (or so it seemed for some time).[12] (In this sense, we might imagine the end of *Great Expectations*— the one in which Pip never sees "the shadow of another parting" from Estella—as the beginning of a "How I Met Your Mother" story).[13] Or, to put it another way, you never will "meet" your mother—or, as all these stories including Brownlow's insist, though you may meet her, you will never know her as I (or your father, or I in the place of your father) knew her: young, and with you not yet born—the mother who is not yet the mother. *Oliver Twist* stages a series of displacements, enactments of the family romance, in which the mother or mother-figure is found wanting (the stock construction is "stained") and replaced with another version; the text moves from Agnes to Nancy and finally to the ethereal Rose, whose slight taint renders her worthy of playing the role of Oliver's quasi-mother, as in aunt or sister. (This ethereality is reproduced in the ending of the TV series, in which the mother is no sooner found than she falls ill and dies, becoming, in effect, an angel). The marriage of Henry and Rose—the high-born gentleman and the slightly tainted angel—is a re-vision and a do-over (a structure discussed in the second half of this chapter), a fantasy version of the marriage of Oliver's own parents.

3. The show erases class as an explicit issue, replacing it with love; all the characters belong to a vague, universalized middle class, in which the possession of jobs or money, clothing, housing, and leisure time, may be discussed but is never in question.

4. In bold opposition to its title, the show unabashedly positions the masculine figure, the putative father, at the center of the story. The interpellation of "you" assumes the viewer's

identification with the character doing the meeting, never with the numerous possible "mothers" he encounters. The point is, of course, that however special "you" are, your mother could have been anyone. And since the mother remains a figure of fantasy—a different mother every week, and finally a dead one—she can never disappoint; the mother we don't like can and will always be replaced. (Indeed, *Oliver Twist* contains several revisions of the mother figure, do-overs which both evoke and suggest an attempt to cleanse or rehabilitate the original, tainted mother. Nancy, who plays the role of Oliver's sister at one point, is a convincing likeness of the fallen maternal figure whose "look" evokes an unfulfillable desire to speak to him, and who of course saves him from a life of crime; Rose Maylie, whose taint, like Oliver's, is not her fault but her parents', is an even more purified and sanctified figure, rehabilitated not least by her own knowledge of and shame about her illegitimate origins. In all of these stories, the child's shame is displaced onto the parents, the specter of the impure mother repeatedly evoked, effaced, and reconstituted, while the child encounters a series of substitutions who evoke but are not his mother, whom he will never definitively "meet.")

5. The "meeting" conceit positions an accident at the center of things, while the unnamed "you" combines accident and inevitability in a way that is central to the doubled construction of the realist subject (as realist fantasy). For the point must be both that "your mother" could be anyone, and that "my" meeting with her, though accidental, was the very special accident that gave rise to the very special you. The inevitability, the "you" it had to be, may first have been the love object—the mother who had to be met—but most crucially it is you, the terminus or end product of the story. It had to be you, because it had to be her; it was accidental and yet inevitable; it was necessary and yet barely missed not happening at all. As in realist fiction, as Philip Weinstein writes, the past tense "unfolds doubly: on the one hand, events seem to be freely unfolding in a forward motion, toward an undeclared future. On the other,

events have already unfolded . . . though not yet been narrated. *The unannounced end underwrites the developing coherence of everything prior to it.* This is the crucial coordinating work of the realist narrator" (69; emphasis in original). The retrospective coherence of the narrative reproduces and ensures the coherence of the subject to whom it all leads. Discovering that coherence, the subject experiences "the grandeur of recognition" (70) in a consolidation that Freud, suggestively mapping middle-class psychology onto the realist novel's fantasy of noble origins, aptly named his majesty the Ego.

The affective narrative is not always retrospective, and the "How I Met Your Mother" story, like the endings of many Victorian novels, for many years projected itself into an imaginary future with the viewer as it subject. If one's true parents are located safely in the distant past—and are also, as in Oliver's case, deceased—not to worry, for in the world of accidental inevitability, you can in fact choose your relations. Indeed, in many Victorian novels, the hero's or heroine's actual parents are replaced by a fantasy family composed of the characters he or she, and by this point probably readers as well, have been encouraged to like best. This conglomerate, often accompanied by a baby or small child, signals the movement into the future of the "how I met" scenario, which maintains the narrative's ambiguity by enabling multiple and ambiguous identifications. For though the answer to the well-known question that is the title of a book some of us encountered in childhood—are you my mother?—is now known by the interpellated subject, the baby or child present at a novel's end offers the image of a subject who will need one day to ask it again: who will need to be told the "how I met your mother" story.

This need to relive the erasure of contingency via narrative, with its inevitable ending, is the burden of what Dror Wahrman rightly sees as a middle-class imaginary. Arguing that the rise of the middle class is a myth, Wahrman describes the way we nevertheless keep discovering this narrative, locating it ever more distantly in time—pushing back its origins as if to reinforce its authenticity.[14] For the more substantive the narrative, the more the good qualities said to define the middle-class subject may be seen as truly his: not subject to the vicissitudes of time and place, but guaranteed to surface at any time, anywhere. Pushing our collective history further and further back in time, that is, we find that our sense of specialness, our individuality, is no accident, but is rather our inheritance: the reliable result of our affective lineage.

2. THE MAYOR OF CASTERBRIDGE AND THE FAILURE OF CONVENTION

Realistic fiction depends on the distinctness of those boundaries [between reality and illusion].

Leo Bersani, *A Future for Astyanax*

Narrative makes the substitution of succession for identity that Hume says we make in attributing personal identity to ourselves. Narrative sequence and the fiction of personal identity are interchangeable.

John Bender, *Imagining the Penitentiary*

Thomas Hardy's *The Mayor of Casterbridge* undermines the sense of specialness with which *Oliver Twist* imbues the realist subject. For instance: when the character called Elizabeth-Jane returns to Casterbridge with her mother Susan to seek out the man she knows only as a relative named Henchard, that character turns out not to be the Elizabeth-Jane we as readers and Henchard too (who considers himself her father) imagine her to be, but another Elizabeth-Jane altogether: a second child, born after the death of the first, to Susan and the sailor Newson—the man to whom Henchard sold his wife one drunken night in a furmity tent. A discontinuity in the text—an eighteen-year gap in the narrative's recounting of events—reinforces, readers later learn, a discontinuity in identity: during the period in which Henchard becomes mayor and Susan lives with Newson, the first child (the original Elizabeth-Jane) has died, and another has been born. The character who thereafter goes by the name of Elizabeth-Jane is thus not the character we meet at the novel's beginning, sold along with her mother to Newson at the furmity tent, but is in fact Newson's own child, born after the death of the previous—the first—Elizabeth-Jane. She is born, it seems, to be secondary: a replacement, a substitute for another child.

The novel thus renders the issue of secondariness both structural and thematic; indeed, it renders the thematic—the affective or identity-shaping components of secondariness—a function of the structural. And it suggests in doing so the inevitable secondariness of character, and indeed of personhood as well: Elizabeth-Jane's arrival to fill a pre-determined slot for a character named Elizabeth-Jane merely reinforces the way in which the role of a character, like that of any family member, is to fill an already-existing slot or position. In the plot of a novel, as in the ideological construction of the social, character, the novel seems to say, is subordinate to system. With its emphasis on secondariness, arbitrariness, and lateness—not only in the case of Elizabeth-Jane, but in other parts of the plot as well—Hardy's novel makes us aware of the way the form of the novel, and especially the realist novel, with its ostensible reproduction of (and secondary relation to) the actual social world, calls upon individuals (in sharp contrast to the distinctiveness the term "individuality," or indeed, in this novel, character, suggests) to function *as* "characters": as place holders in a system, figures who are, insofar as they possess characteristics that enable them to fill a certain slot, interchangeable.[15]

Mayor abounds with episodes—and a general feeling—of belatedness, lateness, secondariness. If Jopp's lateness for his appointment with Henchard, for instance, opens the space in Henchard's employment and in the novel's architecture for Farfrae, the second Elizabeth-Jane, in her very belatedness and secondariness (she is second to her mother in Henchard's universe and second to Lucetta in Farfrae's) reinforces the alignment of secondariness with the note of habitual disappointment—the habitual disappointment of realism—on which the novel ends.[16] The view of life as a temporal construction in which "happiness is but the occasional episode in a general drama of pain"[17]—the condition of Elizabeth-Jane's existence—comes, during the course of the novel, to be identified with a knowledge of the inevitable secondariness or belatedness of the self. Indeed, Henchard's tragedy consists of a coming-to-awareness of that knowledge: the awareness that he himself, someone whose prominence forces what appears as, and what he believes to be, his specialness, his individuality, into view, is just as susceptible to replacement as those, like Elizabeth-Jane, who know themselves to already be replacements, inscribed in a do-over narrative not of their own construction. Henchard's disillusionment is thus a kind of allegory of the way in which the two different views of realist character reconciled by coincidence in *Oliver Twist* once again clash with one another: in one, each character is singular, unique, and special; in the other, he or she is a place-holder, someone who fills a role in a pre-existing system.

"To shake loose from one's wife; to discard that drooping rag of a woman, with her mute complaints and maddening passivity; to escape not by a slinking abandonment but through the public sale of her body to a stranger ... to wrest, through sheer amoral willfulness, a second chance out of life—it is with this stroke, so insidiously attractive to male fantasy, that *The Mayor of Casterbridge* begins."[18] And so, to my mind notoriously, begins Irving Howe's essay on Hardy's novel. Leaving aside any possible distinction between regressive male fantasy and fantasy per se—indeed, assuming that they are the same—Howe fantasizes Hardy's response to critics of this novel's realism: critics who claimed that such a thing as a wife-sale could not happen in actual life. "Had he lived a few decades later than he did," writes Howe, "Hardy might have argued that the opening scene of the novel, partly because it does rest on a firm historical foundation, embodies a mythic kind of truth. Speaking to the depths of common fantasy, it summons blocked desires and transforms us into secret sharers" (384).

Had we as Howe's readers, not to say Hardy's as well, imagined— indeed, wished—that Howe's appeal to "common fantasy" might be assigned to that convenient repository of undesirable knowledge known as the ironic, that possibility is sadly dispelled by his enlisting of readers as secret sharers: his assumption, presumed to be ours as well, that the desire to "shed" one's wife is so deep-seated as to possess the status of myth; his assertion that there exists a universal desire to do so, making room for what he represents as an inevitable and necessary moment in the masculine life-cycle: a "second chance."

But what is exceptionally vertiginous about the novel's beginning may not be uncertainty about whether such things as wife selling actually happened—the question of the relation between historical fact and novelistic realism that Hardy addresses in his preface—but rather the shock the episode delivers to normative views of marriage and conventional ideas of good behavior, momentarily stripping away any illusions a reader might have held about both, either in actual life or in novelistic representation. Leaving aside the obvious sexism of Howe's remarks, I want to take up the issue of the startling nature of the novel's opening itself: a shock based, as are many of the novel's subsequent stagings of events (and other moments in Hardy's fiction), on an absolute failure of conventions and conventionality to constrain or otherwise regulate behavior. The opening of *Mayor* offers an image of conventions out of control, forgotten, not working in the manner they are designed to work. By "conventions" and "conventionality" I mean not just the convention of marriage, which does not in our modern understanding (not according to the historical examples Hardy cites to substantiate his realism, that is) include the option of wife-selling, but also the traditional conventions of the realist novel, which parallel those of the family by providing readers with images of familiarity and comfort, limning the rules and boundaries that make ordinary life navigable, reproducing its characteristic and seemingly immutable (part of that comfort) shape and feel. In this case, novelistic conventions echo marriage rules by failing to provide what those rules ordinarily do provide, what their purpose is to provide: a sense of comfort and solidity. At the beginning of *Mayor*, that is, conventions fail to save: they fail to save us, just as they fail to save Susan and Elizabeth-Jane, from the disorienting disruption of the wife-sale, a disruption of familial bonds and expectations and a violation of what, in fact, conventions are—an adherence to ideas of common human nature defined by forms of accepted behavior.[19] The issue is not just that the novel begins with an ending—the ending of a marriage—or that it begins with a surprise. It is also that the shocking failure of the marriage bond, in either its legal or affective capacity, to prevent the sale from happening—a failure of convention to exert any influence or display any power, to "do" anything—seems to underlie, be strengthened by, and simultaneously strengthen a sense that realist conventions have also been disrupted, that they fail to function as they ordinarily do. Is the marriage's breakup, the "shedding" of a wife by a husband, a fantasy, as Howe proposes? Or is it the convention of marriage itself—the idea of a religious, legal, and presumable affective bond—that is here exposed as fantasy, the result of a belief only briefly held and conveniently maintained—maintained until the moment its inconvenience exceeds its convenience? At stake is not so much a question of the breakdown of a distinction between reality and illusion as the momentary irruption, into the real, of a wish or fantasy that is also presented as "realistic": a breaking of rules that both takes for granted and calls into question the very rules it breaks.

In his preface to *Mayor*, Hardy answers critics of his realism by citing the historical real, pointing out that wife sales were at one time commonplace. Turning aside the idea of fantasy, at least in this way—giving the name "realism" to what would otherwise be unbelievable—the novel works to close the gap, or series of gaps, it has itself opened up.[20] And yet this move is in keeping with the narrative's general tendency to produce gaps or absences with which it, and readers, must contend: to rely on a reader's sense that such a gap has arisen. Indeed, the novel's characteristic structure is the repeated opening of gaps that bring its conventions into view, and call its realism—not just the historical real, but also the belief in the continuity of identity on which novelistic realism relies—into question. In both of these ways, Hardy's strategies define realist fiction as a secondary form. But he also shows that both of these kinds of secondariness—that of structure or convention, on the one hand, and that of character on the other—evoke a desire for, as well as a belief in, their permanence and solidity.

The novel's opening plays with the ways in which what is generally understood as the real is sustained by social conventions, making clear that what characters accept as the condition of their existence is merely the result of a shifting belief in the priority of one convention over another. Henchard's offer to sell his wife is rendered "real" by the sight of cash on the table; "the sight of real money" proves to the crowd that Henchard's proposal is "real in earnest" (12). The money, affirming the reality of the sale, seems to trump any lingering belief in the ability of marriage, as another kind of conventional transaction, to outweigh it: given "real" money, one can, it seems, sell one's wife. Structured so as to expose the "reality" behind the convention of marriage, the scene's emphasis on conventions is reinforced by the sounds of the auction in the background, a social and ideological context that not only renders visible, as many critics suggest, the structure of exchange on which the institution of marriage rests, but also seems to disclose the emotional truth of relations between Susan and Henchard.

The shock of the novel's beginning brings the structure of realism into view as a series of conventions and a filling-in of gaps or blanks: the fulfillment of pre-existing forms (such as marriage) with specific but interchangeable individuals. Picking up on the way in which realism is always in the business of filling in gaps, spaces it has itself created (the form of the usual, the conventional) with something "like" what had previously filled them, the novel points toward the inevitable secondariness of those who occupy such spaces (and the novel's title refers to that secondariness by giving priority to a function—"mayor"—over any particular occupant of that office). Calling attention, throughout the course of the novel, to the secondary or belated—the figure who comes in late—Hardy also calls attention to the arbitrariness and yet crucial importance of position: the spaces and structures that make up the forms of realist fiction and the social arrangements it both supports and affirms. Within this system, it becomes the function of individuals—characters and readers—to fill in, or occupy, those spaces and structures, thereby supporting a particular society's reality by following its conventions. Doing so reinforces the "reality" of these structures—and the realist fantasy they sustain—but also affirms the secondariness, or arbitrariness, of any individual within it.

The wife sale, offering the opportunity for what Howe calls a "second chance," interrupts what, in ordinary life, tends to be imagined as continuous—the state of marriage—stopping and seemingly ending it at one point; attempting to restart it, to do it over, at another. A similar disruption takes place around the identity of Elizabeth-Jane, and, more generally, around the career of Henchard, whose desire to "start again" prompts the wife-sale at the novel's beginning and appears again at its end. *Mayor* thus both stages and exposes, by interrupting, readerly expectations about the relation between sequence and identity. If, according to accepted conventions of realism, in this case as outlined classically by Ian Watt, a proper name alludes to the continuity of character—suggesting, again, the status of realism as a structure of positions to be filled—knowledge of the replacement of one child by another does the same, juxtaposing the shock of difference with an exposure of the power of expectations (in this case, expectations about sequence and continuity, ours as well as Henchard's) to shape belief (just as readers tend to believe the story of Oliver's lineage even as they find it to be unbelievable). What John Bender, citing Hume, refers to as the substitution of succession for identity takes over, with respect to the validity of marriage as well as the continuity of character (37). Conventions, such as Susan's belief that she is married to Henchard and then to Newson, remain in place until they are dislodged by other, more powerful ideas: a process that defines the apparent solidity or permanence of any convention as realist fantasy.

The wife-sale is quickly followed by two Rip Van Winkle-like gaps: the first, when Henchard awakens to knowledge of what he has done the day before, and to the absence of Susan and Elizabeth-Jane—and the second, when the reader, along with the two women, "returns" to find that Henchard has become mayor. These gaps play with the conventional alignment between character and the continuity of identity, offering readers a temporal gap where the conventional narrative of Henchard's rise, along with the story of Susan, Newson, and Elizabeth-Jane might have been: a missing eighteen years. And if there is no doubt that we are meant to accept the post-gap Henchard as identical to the previous one, the same cannot be said of Elizabeth-Jane: the character who returns is not the one who left, but a replacement or substitute for the dead child of the same name. And yet the novel relies on our own, as well as Henchard's, belief in a realist fantasy of character in the form of continuity across these gaps: since the child who died had no prominent features—for readers, no *character*—it is not inconceivable that the figure who replaces her, the character we come to know, is in fact the same as the one who left. (In this sense the emptiness of Oliver's character is also an example of characterological secondariness: his specialness must be and is affirmed by the bonds of affection around him; he himself is an effect of those bonds.) This structure also suggests that repetition—in this case, the form of marriage—creates, even as it gives the lie to, the real; if Henchard's replacement by Newson creates a "false" family, in the sense that Newson is not "really" Elizabeth-Jane's father (or, for that matter, Susan's husband), the death of the first child and birth of a second creates a second family in which Newson's claim to fatherhood bests Henchard's: he really *is* the father of the child. The do-over, in this instance, at least partially fulfills the fantasy of family: if not an actual husband, Newson is nevertheless an actual father. Here as elsewhere in the novel, the structure of the family exerts an ideological force which the narrative, or the novel's "real" world, both obeys and undoes: the space left by Henchard is filled by Newson; the space left by the first Elizabeth-Jane is filled by the second. For if the second Elizabeth-Jane, like the sight of money on the table, makes that character, along with the family structure she inhabits, "real," she also affirms the secondary status of its members. Elizabeth-Jane is always and inevitably a substitute or correction for a missing original, a character replacing another who possesses the same name, their position in the novel's plot—the continuity between Elizabeth-Janes—more important than any possible personality difference (and this issue is never addressed by the text, nor does there seem to be any significant difference in physical appearance, as if age cancels any continuity that might have existed in a single character) might have been. In capitalism as in realism, structure remains intact—certifying itself by means of its own steadfastness—as the occupants of specific positions come and go; structures or conventions appear to possess a power beyond that of any individual character, summoning individual persons according to their requirements.[21] Indeed, the scene in which Henchard contemplates the Elizabeth-Jane he now knows to be someone else's child emphasizes her identity as a position-holder in a genealogical system whose historical "layers" become visible as she sleeps.[22]

The second Elizabeth-Jane is, for readers, a substitute: a daughter whose name designates her continuity with, and status as, a replacement for the child who died. But she is also a character for whom secondariness becomes a crucial form of experience: she is secondary to her father, whose attention moves toward characters better able to satisfy his own compelling needs; to Lucetta, who plays the role of enviable friend as well as substitute or step-mother; to Farfrae, who focuses on her briefly as a potential love-interest before turning his attention to Lucetta. Indeed, secondariness is a widespread condition in the novel: a feeling of coming in late, of belatedness, is something like the human condition in *Mayor*, more prevalent than realist individuality, as in the identification of Henchard as "a man of character."[23] Character or "personal identity" yields to a general subordination to the various structures to which characters belong: here, importantly, the family, including such positions as father and child; almost of equal importance, the novel, which assists in the invention and perpetuation of the idea of "character" itself. Elizabeth-Jane, Farfrae, and Henchard too enact their own secondariness, internalizing the forms, both societal and ideological, in which they take their places. The return of a character named Elizabeth-Jane, along with her mother, confronts us with a realist fantasy—the alignment between a belief in continuity or sequence and a belief in personal identity—but the temporal gap between the first Elizabeth-Jane's departure and the second one's appearance exposes the fragility of the structures on which realist character tends to rely.

And yet if the suggestion of interchangeability between the two reflects, as Genevieve Abravanel persuasively argues, capitalism's logic of exchange, it also puts pressure on the idea of character, accounting for its status as Henchard's last, best, and only claim to distinction. Indeed, distinctive character functions in the novel not as a benefit but as a blocking mechanism: it is precisely what is not wanted, what is not efficacious, in the culture and society of Casterbridge. If the wife sale is the event that generates the entire novel, setting all subsequent events in motion, the impulse behind the sale is what Howe calls Henchard's desire for a second chance: the desire not to be the nobody he feels he is; the desire to fulfill an ambition frustrated, he feels, by marriage. The fantasy that results in shedding his wife, that is, is prompted by another sort of fantasy: the idea that the nobody he is as her husband can be transformed into a somebody without her. And yet Henchard's distinctiveness is precisely what his culture rejects, preferring the flexibility of the man or woman who can fit his or her character to an available position.

Henchard's meeting with Farfrae recalls the structure of the family romance, in which a nobody's encounter with a somebody provokes a dissatisfaction with self that spurs social mobility. Indeed, from this perspective the family-romance scenario becomes an objective correlative for Henchard's insecurities and sense of inferiority: such a character will always meet someone "superior" to himself. But the structure of such a meeting also captures the family romance's characteristic blending of accident and inevitability: the way in which an encounter between members of different classes is, as I argued in the first part of this chapter, both accidental and unavoidable. The meeting of the two, so crucial in the lives of both characters, is a version of the accident that always happens; the significance of the encounter lies in the importance, both immediate and eventual, of their social difference. What Henchard sees in Farfrae—the ability to suit the available position, to fill the empty slot—is not a man of character but rather the opposite: an embodiment of skills, a figure in whom "character" is subordinate to system. The desire and admiration Farfrae evokes is a class effect: an admiration for a difference that takes shape as adaptability and mobility.[24]

One of the novel's other instigating and underlying fantasies—crucial in shaping Henchard's trajectory—is the idea of the second chance, or do-over: Henchard's belief that he can "shed" not only a wife, but the daughter, the family, and the existence that had accompanied them, and in doing so start his life anew. This idea also exposes and challenges conventional alignments of life-trajectory and realist form: just as the novel begins with the declaration of an ending, so too does it end with Henchard's desire for a second (or perhaps third) beginning. That desire, provoked by space and place, appears as Henchard finds himself, at the novel's end, at the same geographical spot from which he entered Casterbridge. But the idea of a second chance or do-over, drawing on ideas of exchange and iterability that appear elsewhere in the novel (the duplication of Elizabeth-Jane; the reproduction of images of Henchard and Lucetta), takes shape here as the imagined exchange of life itself: as if, as in the idea of selling one's wife, one can trade in one life for another version, with a life or career trajectory imagined as only one in a series of possible options.[25]

The debilitating effect of the idea of character on Henchard, and the competitiveness that structures his relation to Farfrae as well as that between Elizabeth-Jane and Lucetta, are the products of a system so informed by a competitive ethos that it seems "character" is something only one person in any given structure or context can possess. Hence the novel's subtitle, "A Man of Character," may refer less to particular qualities that contribute to Henchard's downfall—his willfulness or stubbornness—then to the possession of character itself, in the sense that any individual in possession of one might consider him or herself to be irreplaceable, distinctive, one of a kind. If Henchard's story has the feeling of a tragic fall, as readers have often suggested, his fatal flaw may be not the nature of his character but his belief in the uniqueness of character per se, including the conviction that rather than give way to another person—another hay trusser, another mayor—he may himself start over, persisting indefinitely in a series of reinventions.

The Mayor of Casterbridge is, of course, a "how I met your mother" story, but one in which the conventional has become fully unconventional: from Elizabeth-Jane's point of view, her father's history tells not how I met your mother but how I left your mother, how I abandoned your mother, indeed, bizarrely, how I sold your mother—not the story conventionally told, but a nightmare version of what might happen after the family romance has ended, after the conventional pattern has been followed. Indeed, it is the story of what might happen *as a result of* following the conventional pattern: of sticking doggedly to the conventions of marriage and family. Refocusing the narrative in this manner makes Elizabeth-Jane its second person in two ways: the object or addressee of the narrative, she also exemplifies the inevitable secondariness of the realist subject—even, and perhaps especially, of the realist subject who feels, because he is a realist subject, that he should be first. Responding to the call of Althusser's disciplinary institutions in their various forms, however—the social system, the realist novel, the family—the subject is necessarily a place-filler, an addressee, the occupier of a position: the product of a series of invitations whose own fantasmatic status is not customarily or conventionally made visible.

Chapter 3

Castles in the Air

Trollope's Realist Fantasy

A scene in Trollope's *Orley Farm* (1862) seems almost dreamlike in its literalization of the constraints that typically hamper the freedom of characters in realist novels. Felix Graham has injured himself falling from a horse while visiting his friend Staveley and is invited to recuperate in Staveley's house. He is in love with Staveley's sister Madeline and his friend disapproves of the connection, but the convalescence puts the two in close proximity. Confined to his sickbed, Graham cannot leave the room; propriety keeps Madeline from entering, though she does stop at the threshold to speak to him. His injury leaves him no choice but to observe the restrictions Staveley has imposed upon him ("The offer of a further asylum in the seclusion of that bedroom had been made to him by his friend with a sort of proviso that it would not be well that he should go further than the bedroom"): he can daydream but he cannot act.[1] The question he asks himself—why should he not propose marriage to Madeline Staveley?—is answered by the basic facts of the situation: his injury literalizes and renders mandatory the observance of friendship and the more general proprieties that would prevent him, should he choose to be prevented, from doing so. And yet of course (another aspect of the scene's dreaminess) these constraints—the strictures of friendship and of good behavior—are undermined as well as reinforced by his immobility. From his sickroom Graham has little to do but fantasize, little to do but listen for "the footfall of Madeline Staveley's step" (I:334). The question of why he should not (see her, talk to her, marry her) inevitably arises, his enforced immobility disrupting the prohibitions that themselves go no small way toward inciting daydreaming. The offer and the "sort of proviso" that conditions it, that is, lead to a familiar Trollopian spectacle: a character wondering about what he or she should or should not do; an extended meditation about possibilities and probabilities. In this scene such thinking takes shape in the form of a peculiarly negative but distinctively Trollopian question: "why should he not?" "Why might he not aspire to the hand of Madeline Staveley,—he who had been assured that he need regard no woman as too high for his aspirations?" (2:66).

> Why should Madeline Stavely be out of his reach, simply because she was his friend's sister? He had been made welcome to that house, and therefore he was bound to do nothing unhandsome by the family. But then he was bound by other laws, equally clear, to do nothing unhandsome by any other family—or by any other lady. If there was anything in Staveley's words, they applied as strongly to Staveley's sister as to any other girl. And why should not he, as a lawyer, marry a lawyer's daughter? (1:399)

The more universal the prohibition, Graham's argument seems to go, the less it applies to him in particular. His thought process matches each law with an argument against it, each noted "binding" unraveled by a question that seems at once to require a detailed response and to repudiate, as rhetorical questions are bound to do, the need for any answer at all. If the sickroom both literalizes Graham's binding and becomes a site "for the representation of an alternative society and mode of existence," as Miriam Bailin puts it, it makes sense that constraint and its absence are equally matched here, each "why should I not" inviting argument and simultaneously suggesting that nothing will deter the questioner from doing what he wants.[2] Rather than constrain his fantasy, his situation proves a perfect venue for it: an opportunity to nurse, coddle, and feed it.

More than is usual in Trollope's fiction, something about this scene seems dreamlike. The issue is not that Graham is fantasizing, for though "why should I not" is a fantasy question, the daydream itself—of marrying his friend's sister—can hardly be said to violate the boundaries of realist convention. Rather, the scene seems overdetermined: the injury; the small room; the regressive suggestion of the sickroom and the need to be nursed; the fact of being positioned in temptation's way but explicitly forbidden to give in to it; the presence of passageways and thresholds—all suggest the generic elements of a classic good dream.[3] It is as if, in detaching this character from ordinary realist conditions via the special circumstances of his injury, the scene also presents his situation as a figure for those conditions: for the characteristic binding of the realist character by laws, prohibitions, and proprieties. Trollope does something here that he does not often do: rather than daydream according to realist conventions, as Peter Allen has described the novelist's youthful practice, he seems to be dreaming of them.[4]

Trollope's autobiography includes an account of his own pleasure, even ecstasy, in the imagining of characters:

> I have wandered alone among the rocks and woods, crying at their grief, laughing at their absurdities, and thoroughly enjoying their joy. I have been impregnated with my own creations till it has been my only excitement to sit with the pen in my hand, and drive my team before me at as quick a pace as I could make them travel. (176)

It describes as well the habit of mental storytelling I have already discussed: a process that he called the building of "castles in the air" and described as training for novel-writing, situating the kind of fantasy described above in the context of order and rule.

> For weeks, for months, if I remember rightly, from year to year, I would carry on the same tale, binding myself to certain laws, to certain proportions, and proprieties, and unities. . . . I learned in this way to maintain an interest in a fictitious story, to dwell on a work created by my own imagination, and to live in a world altogether outside the world of my own material life. In after years I have done the same,—with this difference, that I have discarded the hero of my early dreams, and have been able to lay my own identity aside. (143)

These passages describe several key qualities of Trollope's realism: his emotional investment in characters of his own devising; his suggestion of an apparent loss of control—laughing and crying—balanced by an assertion of control: "driv[ing] my team before me." Indeed, the idea of "practicing" daydreaming—returning day after day to the same tale—brings these two qualities together, suggesting that daydreaming according to realist conventions meant for Trollope something that seems to run counter to the very nature of fantasy: the ability to believe in his imaginative productions without wholly giving in to their "reality"; the attempt to maintain control of the narrative through adherence to the laws, proportions, and proprieties by means of which he defined his own realist project. The binding nature of these conventions, Trollope suggests, enabled him to produce the characters his contemporaries, and he himself, found so compellingly realistic, and perhaps contributed as well to his overarching topics: the tension between individual desire and social constraint; the moral and ethical quandaries his characters regularly face. And since his characters are bound not only to the social conventions and institutions whose effects realist fiction typically explores but also to particular novelistic conventions, the question "why should I not" becomes one of genre as well as of behavior. What a character can or cannot do according to realist conventions, that is, functions as a form of binding—a "sort of proviso"—that might be seen as the equivalent of, and as overlapping with, the socially-imposed prohibitions with which realism is typically concerned. Like the prohibitions that confine Felix Graham to his sickroom, they provide an enabling structure, and indeed a template, for the production of that paradoxical thing I am calling realist fantasy.[5]

Graham's self-questioning or daydreaming, framed by the question, "Why should I not?" belongs to a category widely discussed in Trollope's fiction under such names as rationalization, ratiocination, or simply argument: an extended period of thinking, meditating, and/ or strategizing in which both characters and narrator engage. Walter Kendrick calls it "conscious thinking" and "self-dialogue"; Amanda Anderson points out "[T]he great attention paid in his novels to subjective thought processes and interpersonal interactions, and the way the narrative consideration of such matters seems to expand and dilate in an autotelic way, as though plot has been utterly abandoned." Rebecca Richardson describes a language structured by comparison and competition ("we find that the comparative language so ubiquitous in this novel is not only the narrator's style, but also the style of his characters"), while Mary Poovey writes that this thinking process is one in which characters judge one another as the narrator judges them, and as readers judge their neighbors in ordinary life.[6] I want to discuss here a subset of this activity, a form of thinking I will call, following Trollope's lead, the building of castles in the air, in which characters model the kind of cogitation Trollope describes as having produced them. In this structure, characters are represented as subjecting impulse or fantasy to a mental practice that resembles Trollope's description of his own "practice"—a term that does double-duty here—for preparing to write realist novels. This particular kind of thinking includes an anticipatory, meditative fantasizing about the "proprieties" or conventions that might constrain the advancing of a character's wishes (thus it matters, as it often does in Trollope, that Graham's marriage hopes are aspirational in more ways than one, since Madeline is above him in social status): a process that, though framed as a consideration of prohibitions (why should I not?) in fact allows the fantasy to take shape. It also includes, like Trollope's notorious descriptions of his writing practice, a concern with the material circumstances within which that thinking takes place, over and above a concern with its content.

My point is not that the language of characters echoes that of the narrator (though I do want to argue that narrator, characters, and, in Trollope's projection of them, readers as well engage in this activity), nor that fiction exists as a dramatization of abstract argument, substituting "the concrete contours of a subtly varied landscape for the moral philosopher's one-dimensional map."[7] Rather, I want to suggest that when Trollope represents many of his characters and projects his readers as well as engaging in a version of his own proto-novelistic activity, he foregrounds what I am calling the novels' realist fantasy: that structure within which an author's use of particular conventions both enables individual fantasies and itself constitutes the more general and generalized fantasy that makes up his or her imagining of the real. Within this context, constructing castles in the air is imagined as constitutive of everyday life not just for Trollope, but for his characters and readers as well, in a manner that, like the author's own career, links spectacles of aristocratic leisure with the aspirational structure of middle-class labor. *Orley Farm* is particularly appropriate for this investigation for several reasons. The novel devotes an unusual amount of attention not just to the thoughts of characters—an attention that appears everywhere in Trollope—but to a particular kind of thinking that resembles Trollope's account of his own daydreaming. The "secret" of the novel's plot is revealed early, accompanied by the anti-sensation rhetoric that, also commonplace in Trollope, appears in a different light when we consider the kind of thinking that castle-building represents. And, finally, the novel contains numerous examples of characters asking themselves, "Why should I not?"

The realist character may always in some way resemble the injured fellow in the sickroom, bound by physical constraints generally taken for granted; by moral ones frequently brought to bear; by proprieties in the form of the demands of friendship and manners or the opinions of others; by laws and, as Graham puts it, other laws—a condition Nicholas Dames has described as the "wounding, even tragic split between what an individual wants and what that individual's practical social options might be."[8] Bound by conventions of all kinds, it is not surprising that such a character might be imagined or even imagine himself inhabiting, if only briefly, an alternative realm, beyond the one that routinely seeks to immobilize him. Indeed, such imagining sometimes takes shape in realist fiction as a shift to another genre, conveying a sense that the fulfillment of a character's desires—the taking of steps that may involve leaping over strictures of propriety, law, and friendship, for example— must be facilitated by non-realist means and take place in a non-realist context, outside the rules that govern ordinary life.

It has posed no problem for critical classification that novelists known as realists, including George Eliot and Charlotte Brontë, often include elements of other genres—usually romance or the Gothic— within their own borders. At the end of Eliot's *Middlemarch* the novel's dominant realist mode gives way to a melodramatic matching of internal and external weather; toward the end of *Jane Eyre* a mysterious telepathy enables Jane Eyre to hear Rochester's call. More specifically, canonical novels classified as realist (*Adam Bede* among them) sometimes evoke non-realist genres to express particular characters' fantasies. In doing so, they align the breaking of social rules with the crossing of generic boundaries, as if characters need to learn not only how to adhere to social laws but must also be reminded to stay within (or leave behind, as the culminating scene between Dorothea and Will in *Middlemarch* suggests) the boundaries of their own genre. The implication is that fantasy cannot be accommodated within the genre of the realist novel: that the fantasizing character must go elsewhere to indulge his or her desires. The evocation of other genres or modes within the framework of realist fiction has traditionally been associated with realism's tendency to be defined, and to define itself, in opposition to them: "I am realistic. My friend Wilkie Collins is generally supposed to be sensational," Trollope writes, concluding, "[A] good novel should be both, and both to the highest degree" (*Autobiography* 227). This strategy reinforces the apparent realism of the conventions by means of which these novels convey their characteristic effects, in a sleight of hand that, highlighting the conventionality of other genres, makes the more "realist" parts of a novel—those not making use of the characteristic tropes of romance or the Gothic, for instance—appear to be convention-free.

Constituting distinct romances, Gothic scenarios, or melodrama within their own borders, realist novels scapegoat them along with the modes of thinking and feeling with which they are associated without (apparently) compromising their own principles, responding to the presence of another genre—as if to an invading foreign body—with a punitive drama of expulsion. Readers too are disciplined for their attachments to non-realist conventions: attachments the novels themselves provisionally encourage.[9] When Eliot embeds a romance—the seduction of Hetty Sorrel by Arthur Donnithorne—within the framework of *Adam Bede,* she warns readers away from it by a clear attention to generic markers: the sense that both the novel and this plot's key players convey (with different degrees of understanding) that they are meeting in an otherworldly, fairy-tale context. But when Dickens's *Great Expectations* ties Pip's ambitions to a fairy-tale plot whose falseness must be revealed to expose a grim reality, Pip's own misguided beliefs about the source of his inheritance are aligned with those of readers who, with the novel's encouragement, have been misled along with him. Readers are chastised, that is, for having been seduced not just by identifying with Pip's desires, but for having temporarily followed the rules—accepted the conventions—of another genre.

In Trollope's novels, on the contrary, fantasy appears wholly as a realist affair (writes Kendrick, "In Trollope's theory, poetry and romance designate territories outside the boundaries of the realist novel"; 71). Despite the dreaminess of the scene with which this chapter begins, Trollope's fiction overwhelmingly takes shape in what Christopher Herbert has called a "stringently" realistic mode in which genres other than realism have already been disallowed, his novelistic universe, we might say, pre-disillusioned, both formally (with reference to strategies of representation) and thematically (with reference to content).[10] If disillusionment, the affective mode for which novelistic realism is known, involves immersing characters and readers in a fantasy that ends with its dismantling (again, *Great Expectations* is the classic example in British fiction), Trollope's realism projects a world in which individual fantasies or illusions tend to be accompanied by a detailed exposition of the numerous reasons why they cannot or should not be acted upon: an extended thinking-through of the practical conditions that render their fulfillment undesirable or impossible. In this process, there is no place for the fantastical possibilities of romance or the Gothic—no leap to another genre that might allow realist disillusionment to be forestalled. Romance takes place within the realm of the ordinary, as in Felix Graham's case, despite that scene's dreamy touches. The possibility of marriage between Sir Peregrine and Lady Mason (also in *Orley Farm*), or of an affair between that same lady and her lawyer, receive varying degrees of detailed exposition: not so much a disillusioning as a pre-disillusioning—an elaboration, within the character's own thinking, of the real-world difficulties a particular fantasy entails. This type of thinking or fantasizing is one of the forms Trollope's realism takes: it is both a product and a dramatization of daydreaming within the boundaries of realist conventions. Indeed, we might say, fantasy in Trollope only appears in the form of *fantasizing*, and, more specifically, fantasizing about the kinds of conditions, prohibitions, and proprieties (to use Trollope's terms for describing his daydreams) that might interfere with a character's desires. If other novels define fantasy as a form of escape from the real by setting it within an alternative set of conventions, Trollope by contrast subjects impulses or fantasies to intense mental scrutiny, a detailed articulation of their relation to the real. It is in this context that the question "why should I not?" proves exemplary.[11]

Why should I (or she, or he) not, asked implicitly or explicitly, might be described as a quintessentially Trollopian question. For instance: nothing happens—nothing narratable—in Trollope's first novel, *The Warden* (1855), until that novel's central character, Mr. Harding, discovers that he has long been doing something he perhaps should not have done: he has been the recipient of an income from his duties at Barchester's hospital far in excess (this is the question the novel raises) of what was due to him under the terms of John Hiram's will.[12] The discovery provokes a series of questions whose purpose is to forward consideration of whether Harding should or should not continue to take the money.

> What right had he [Bold] to say that John Hiram's will was not fairly carried out? But then the question would arise within his heart.—Was that will fairly acted on? Did John Hiram mean that the warden of his hospital should receive considerably more out of the legacy than all the twelve men together for whose behoof the hospital was built? Could it be possible that John Bold was right...? What if it should be proved before the light of day that he, whose life had been so happy, so quiet, so respected, had absorbed £8,000 to which he had no title, and which he could never repay?[13]

The non-narratability of anything earlier might be taken for granted; this discovery is, of course, where the novel begins, the complacency of Mr. Harding's life up until this point alluded to but not detailed, and apparently not requiring elaboration: he was "happy, quiet, respected," the money in question not so much consciously spent as unconsciously "absorbed" (34). To these questions is quickly attached another, explicitly structured as a negative, also involving desire and the prohibitions that attend it: why should Harding's daughter Eleanor not marry John Bold?

The answer is tied to the previous discovery: Bold is the very fellow who, true to his name, has raised the question of the propriety and legality of Mr. Harding's income.

> Nor is there any reason why Eleanor Harding should not love John Bold. He has all those qualities which are likely to touch a girl's heart. He is brave, eager, and amusing; well-made and good-looking; young and enterprising: his character is in all respects good; he has sufficient income to support a wife; he is her father's friend; and, above all, he is in love with her. Then why should not Eleanor Harding be attached to John Bold? (16–17)

What follows, and makes up the substance of the novel, is a record of the progress of Harding's thinking about both of these issues. The possibility of having done wrong and Harding's dawning awareness of that possibility form the justification for and substance of much of the novel; *The Warden* as a whole, that is, represents an answer to the question: why should he not? And though the issue is defined as one Mr. Harding must resolve, "within his heart," to his own satisfaction, it is also fought (thanks to Bold) on the pages of the *Jupiter*. Harding's private feelings are aroused in the first place by, and brought for testing to, the court of public opinion: "He, that shy, retiring man, who had so comforted himself in the hidden obscurity of his lot, who had so enjoyed the unassuming warmth of his own little corner, he was now to be dragged forth into the glaring day, and gibbeted before ferocious multitudes" (127).

The question picks up again, implicitly, at the beginning of *Barchester Towers*, in the context of the seemliness of ambition, as Harding finds himself uncomfortably contemplating the likelihood that on the event of his father's death he might be named bishop. It appears explicitly later in the novel: "If Mr. Harding could not be warden of the hospital, why should he not be Dean of Barchester?"[14] "Why should I not" introduces a period of speculation, a consideration of what is possible and probable, often in the context of an ambition that constitutes a large part of a character's identity; what is striking about it as a question is its foregrounding of prohibition: not why should I, but why should I not? Lady Eustace thinking about whether the law can interfere with her desire to keep the diamonds (*The Eustace Diamonds*); Emily Wharton considering whether to marry Ferdinand Lopez (*The Prime Minister*); Lady Carbury considering her son's marriage (*The Way We Live Now*)—

> Then the heiress herself had accepted her son! If so, surely the thing might be done. Lady Carbury recalled to mind her old conviction that a daughter may always succeed in beating a hard-hearted parent in a contention about marriage, if she be well in earnest. But then the girl must be really in earnest, and her earnestness will depend on that of her lover. In this case, however, there was as yet no reason for supposing that the great man would object. As far as outward signs went, the great man had shown some partiality for her son. No doubt it was Mr. Melmotte who had made Sir Felix a director of the great American Company. Felix had also been kindly received in Grosvenor Square. And then Sir Felix was Sir Felix,—a real baronet. Mr. Melmotte had no doubt endeavoured to catch this and that lord; but, failing a lord, why should he not content himself with a baronet?[15]

—all of these are examples of aspiring characters actively seeking possible constraints, wondering what might prevent their aspirations from playing out as they wish, in a manner that, as in the case of Graham's reflections about Madeline Staveley, constitutes their fantasy's enabling condition.

Indeed, Why should I not? is the question one might imagine enabling Trollope's own fantasy of authorship as his *Autobiography* describes it, since its opening chapters detail a series of conditions that might very well prevent an uneducated, socially-excluded boy from becoming a celebrated novelist. *An Autobiography* is full of reasons why he should not: everything about the childhood suffering Trollope recounts constitutes a prohibition against the glories he eventually gained—providing not only an account of why he should not, but an explanation of why in all likelihood he probably would not. The story of *An Autobiography* is that of the novelist overcoming the obstacles of his early life by dint of daydreaming and hard work, and it represents daydreaming as the "dangerous" practice that made such overcoming possible: "I have explained, when speaking of my school-days, how it came to pass that other boys would not play with me. I was therefore alone, and had to form my plays within myself. . . . There can, I imagine, hardly be a more dangerous mental practice; but I have often doubted whether, had it not been my practice, I should ever have written a novel" (42–43). Arguably taking the danger out of this practice by means of repetition—and thereby transforming fantasy into labor—Trollope nevertheless requires danger to fuel it, and we see the necessity of the "practice" involved in negotiating this relation both in the shape of his characters' stratagems and in the fact that daydreaming according to realist conventions forms a significant part of what they do. In the novels' plots as well as in their production, the practice of thinking through the relation between fantasy and its constraints appears as both content and form, as the novels it produces meditate about the possible fulfillment of desire in the context of the very real constraints of the social world.[16]

In comparison with the dreamlike representation of Felix Graham's sickroom musings, *Orley Farm*'s representation of Sir Peregrine considering whether to propose marriage to Lady Mason conforms to a more starkly observed realist protocol, one that focuses less on introspection and more on the kinds of details Roland Barthes has defined as crucial to realist representation:[17]

> He sat thinking, with his glass of claret untouched by his side, and with the biscuit which he had taken lying untouched upon the table. As he sat he had raised one leg upon the other, placing his foot on his knee, and he held it there with his hand placed upon his instep. And so he sat without moving for some quarter of an hour, trying to use all his mind on the subject which occupied it. At last he roused himself, almost with a start, and leaving his chair, walked three or four times the length of the room. 'Why should I not?' at last he said to himself, stopping suddenly and placing his hand upon the table. 'Why should I not, if it pleases me? It shall

not injure him, nor her.' And then he walked again. 'But I will ask Edith,' he said, still speaking to himself. 'If she says that she disapproves of it, I will not do it.' And then he left the room, while the wine remained untasted on the table. (I:247–48)

Though we are provided with few details about his thoughts, it seems certain that Peregrine, like Graham, imagines nothing outside the bounds of the ordinary, and the bounds of the ordinary are in fact what this description emphasizes: the extent to which Peregrine seems hemmed in or immobilized by his situation is conveyed by the noting of his minute range of motion, measured out in the narrator's attention to the exact placement of his hand; the pacing out of his steps; the detail of his untouched biscuit and wine. In fact, each man is entertaining the same question: why should he not ask the woman he loves to marry him? If Trollope's novels are examples of daydreaming according to realist conventions, both of these scenes might be taken as projections of that very activity, this second one, indeed, not so different in its privileging of externalities over introspection from Trollope's representation of himself writing: "It had at this time become my custom,— and it still is my custom . . . to write with my watch before me, and to require from myself 250 words every quarter of an hour" (*Autobiography* 271–72). And yet despite the differences between these scenes and characters, Felix Graham and Peregrine Orme may both be described as castle builders: in the novel's extended expositions of each spinning a fantasy about his own future; in the representation, in each case, of a man in a room thinking, perhaps daydreaming; in a rhetoric of verbal pictures that juxtapose the possibilities of fantasy with the "binding" or constraints of the real. Thus it makes sense that in displaying the realist novelist bound by his calling—doing his job—as he notes the number of steps; the status of wine and biscuit; the movement of a hand—these scenes bring to mind Trollope's account of his own novelistic production: descriptions of the novelist bound to his desk and tied as well to the other material effects that enable his practice: a table, a chair, a watch. As in Trollope's descriptions of his own activity, the content of characters' thinking is less important in these scenes than the fact that thinking is taking place, and that it occurs regularly and within a specific material framework, wherein a character—here, Sir Peregrine—lays his identity aside as he contemplates his options.

Laying his own identity aside, Trollope filled up much of the space of his novels with characters who, at least in this sense, resemble himself. If in Felix's case we have more interiority and in Peregrine's more exteriority; if in Felix we have a young, not-very-well-off visitor to a friend's estate and in Peregrine a member of the landed aristocracy, it is nevertheless true that both take the time to build castles in the air. This consistency extends, as I will discuss below, to Trollope's readers, who are characteristically chastised (pre-disillusioned) by the Trollopian narrator for desiring the pleasures of sensation fiction: a desire the author both summons and disciplines by dramatizing his refusal to withhold plot details that, he asserts, another kind of novelist would have kept back. He offers instead not only those details—giving his secrets away—but also what might be described as the opposite of sensation fiction's narrative pleasures: the repeated spectacle of characters thinking. Trollope thus projects the image of a community of readers so deeply interested in what his characters are thinking that they are willing to spend a great deal of time watching them doing it, mirroring, as they do so, the characters' own required stillness. Moreover, this mirroring implies, and the narrator himself suggests, this experience may teach readers to fill in the novels' blank spaces with details of their own devising: to themselves become, that is, builders of castles in the air.

As its name suggests, castle-building is structured less by knowledge of any particular facts than by the narrative possibilities the absence of facts provokes.[18] The truth may simply not be known (Peregrine, for instance, believes Lady Mason to be innocent), or actual knowledge of others may be deferred or rendered momentarily irrelevant in the interest of developing the narrative at hand (as in Furnival's desire not to know whether Lady Mason is guilty). "Why should I not" is an apt summary of the way, for instance, the progress of Graham's thoughts ("If there was anything in Staveley's words, they applied as strongly to Staveley's sister as to any other girl. And why should not he, as a lawyer, marry a lawyer's daughter?") is to imagine setting aside his friend's request as he drives his own desires before him. And yet what gives this kind of fantasizing its realist quality is its attention to prohibition (why should I not?): the tempering of fantasy with a dose of reality by giving prohibition pride of place. The castle in the air is, indeed, a fantasy of constraint, in which wishes and desires appear in the context of real-world prohibitions. When Felix Graham and Sir Peregrine Orme daydream according to realist conventions, they weigh their desires against possible obstacles, especially in the form of the imagined opinions of others. Indeed, the difference between what might be called a conventional idea of fantasy as the removal of constraint and the building of castles in the air lies in the latter's inclusion of, indeed insistence on, prohibitions and proprieties: obstacles to be navigated in the contemplation of a character's wishes and desires.

In each case—and there are numerous examples in *Orley Farm*—introspection takes the form of extended speculation in which facts are subordinated to suppositions: narrative possibilities that, as in Trollope's own castle-building, invest other characters and the day-dreamer himself with a certain provisional reality—the reality, we might say, of the dreamer's own desire. What it means to lay one's identity aside in such a context is that this laying aside is already identity's structure: the self projected in narrative as an object of the public eye is not the same as the self asking the question, the self imagining how the scene might play out. The form of the question ("why should I not?") captures a tension between fantasy and prohibition that appears here as a hallmark or exemplary figure for Trollope's realism: part of a more general structure in which fantasy is not another genre but rather a questioning of the limits and boundaries of the social world, a querying of the relation between individual desires and real—as well as realist—conditions. The castle in the air divides the self into a questioner, with his or her wishes and desires, and an imagined public realm within which what Trollope calls "propriety" offers certain kinds of answers. This is the structure required by the aspirational readership of Victorian fiction, an audience acutely attuned to the process of identity-building and especially to the considerations involved in attempting to rise in society: a class for whom the practice of novel reading, especially in the periodicity of its serial form, offered regular practice in the laying-aside of identity in the contemplation of being someone else.

There are reasons why Felix Graham should not marry Madeline Staveley: for one thing, he has prepared a wife for himself in the person of Mary Snow, an orphan whose character he has been "moulding" to suit him; it is also the case that his "low position, in reference to worldly affairs, made any such passion on his part quite hopeless." It is Peregrine Orme, indeed—the younger Peregrine—of whom it is said that there "could be no possible reason why Peregrine Orme should not win and wear the beautiful girl whom he so much admired" (1:227). And yet Peregrine, who has no reasons why he should not, other than the fact that Madeline does not love him, is not the focus of interest. If the obstacles to Graham's happiness disappear in something of a dreamlike manner ("It seems like a dream to me," he says of Madeline's parents, "that they should have accepted me as their son-in-law" [2:352]), more complex versions of the tension between desire and the constraints upon it appear in the situations of the novel's central characters. Peregrine, unable to believe in Lady Mason's guilt, asks himself why he should not propose marriage to her, and, not knowing the reason, proceeds to do so; Mr. Furnival, her lawyer, engages in extended fantasies about his relation to her, asking himself repeatedly why he should not help her if he suspects she is guilty. And the novel's chief castle builder, Lady Mason, the figure at the center of so many of these fantasies, has for twenty years inhabited a castle of her own devising, Orley Farm—as the result of an act accomplished by herself in the dark of night some twenty years previous, at which time, we might imagine, she asked herself, why should I not? and refused to be dissuaded by the answer.

Having become, the narrator tells us, something of a Lothario in his old age, Furnival is at odds with his wife, his home life has become uncomfortable, and the chief pleasures he can currently imagine involve being in Lady Mason's presence.

And as we are searching into his innermost heart we must say more than this. Mrs. Furnival perhaps had no sufficient grounds for those terrible fears of hers; but nevertheless the mistress of Orley Farm was very comely in the eyes of the lawyer. Her eyes, when full of tears, were very bright, and her hand, as it lay on his, was very soft. He laid out for himself no scheme of wickedness with reference to her; he purposely entertained no thoughts which he knew to be wrong; but, nevertheless, he did feel that he liked to have her by him, that he liked to be her adviser and friend, and that he liked to wipe the tears from those eyes—not by a material handkerchief from his pocket, but by immaterial manly sympathy from his bosom; and that he liked also to feel the pressure of that hand. . . . It was very wrong that it should have been so, but the case is not without a parallel. (I:251–52)

If castles in the air depend on not knowing the facts, Furnival creates for himself a position that positively requires him, if he is to continue to assist Lady Mason, not to know what, in his professional capacity, it is his business to know.

It would be sweet to feel that she was in his hands, and that he would treat her with mercy and kindness. But then a hundred other thoughts forbade him to think more of this. If she had been guilty—if she declared her guilt to him—would not restitution be necessary? In that case her son must know it, and all the world must know it. Such a confession would be incompatible with that innocence before the world which it was necessary that she should maintain. Moreover, he must be able to proclaim aloud his belief in her innocence; and how could he do that, knowing her to be guilty—knowing that she also knew that he had such knowledge? It was impossible that he should ask any such questions, or admit of any such confidence. (I:253)

Indeed, the extent to which castle-building takes the place of interaction between characters—interaction that might yield the facts necessary to make decisions—is wonderfully captured in this non-exchange between the two:

By this time, Furnival had dropped the hand, and was sitting still, meditating, looking earnestly at the fire while Lady Mason was looking earnestly at him. She was trying to gather from his face whether he had seen signs of danger, and he was trying to gather

from her words whether there might actually be cause to appre-
hend danger. How was he to know what was actually inside her
mind; what were her actual thoughts and inward reasonings on
this subject; what private knowledge she might have which was
still kept back from him? . . . Could it be possible that anything had
been kept back from him? Were there facts unknown to him, but
known to her, which would be terrible, fatal, damning to his sweet
friend if proved before all the world? He could not bring himself
to ask her, but yet it was so material that he should know! . . . And
now he sat, thinking. . . . (I:118–19)

The danger with which Furnival flirts is not the same as that which
preys on Lady Mason's mind, but the thoughts of both circle around,
and are fueled by, a sense of what they cannot possibly say or do. Can
he defend someone he suspects is guilty? Having done so before, he
decides, he can do so again. But his greatest concern is to clear Lady
Mason not in court, but in the world's eyes: "It was not that he dreaded
the idea of thinking her guilty himself; perhaps he did think her
now—he half thought her so, at any rate; but he greatly dreaded the
idea of others thinking so" (I:250). The best means of promoting both
her interests and his, Furnival concludes, involves fostering certain
opinions: as in the passage above, the novel's chief action, exceeding
the actual trial in its importance, takes place at the level of speculating, attempting to influence, and indeed circulating to one group the
thoughts of another. "It would be a great thing if he could spread abroad
the conviction that she was an injured woman. It would be a great thing
even if he could make it known that the great people of the neighbour-
hood so thought" (I:252).

What allows Furnival to extend his thinking, of course, are the
"hundred other thoughts" he is forbidden to think, and thus his fantasies
of aiding Lady Mason yield to speculations about witnesses, arguments,
and counter-arguments—musings about legal processes so prolonged
that even a novelist in the business of providing readers with numerous
pages of extended ratiocination signals their length by merely announcing, after recounting in detail the lawyer's speculations about the moves
and counter-moves of witnesses, magistrates, and other lawyers, that he

is beginning the process over again. Furnival keeps hold of his fantasy, that is, by transmuting it into professional labor, turning more dangerous thoughts into safer ones—or, at least, into speculations whose particular form of danger fits the contours of his professional identity.

> And then he also sat thinking. Might it not be probable, that, with a little judicious exercise of their memory, those two witnesses would remember that they had signed two documents; or, at any rate, looking to the lapse of the time, that they might be induced to forget altogether whether they had signed one, two, or three? Or even if they could be mystified so that nothing could be proved, it would still be well with his client. Indeed no magistrate would commit such a person as Lady Mason, especially after so long an interval, and no grand jury would find a bill against her, except upon evidence that was clear, well-defined, and almost indubitable. If any point of doubt could be shown, she might be brought off without a trial, if only she would be true to herself. At the former trial there was the existing codicil . . . . And then Mr. Furnival thought it all over again and again. (I:248–49)

Outside a certain framework—having established the kind of thing Furnival is thinking—the novel almost flaunts the lack of necessity for further details; what is important to establish is the continued practice of thinking, the status of thinking as a practice: the decision to conjecture rather than to know; the drawing out of the process of speculating as a routinized activity.[19]

Both Furnival and Peregrine fantasize about Lady Mason in the context of the arena of public perception. Furnival, who suspects why he should not, is in a position to inform his friend, who has no idea, and yet, as in the scene between himself and Lady Mason, he does not, only letting Peregrine know of the suspicions of others. Peregrine, for his own part, has framed his fantasy about Lady Mason as an extension of his fantasy about himself: his intention has always been to marry "a lady who in social life is my equal" (2:40). The immobility of his person as he sits thinking suggests the fixed quality of his thoughts; his investment in his own persona is so crucial to him that when he finds out the truth he rescinds the offer he has already made. Thoroughly subject to rules of propriety, his body as regulated as his mind, Peregrine—after precisely fifteen minutes of cogitation (the same amount of time, Trollope tells us, that he himself requires to write 250 words)—can only come to the conclusion that he had better ask his daughter. More powerfully than Furnival, whose profession affords him a way to work around the issue, Peregrine is overwhelmed by the effect he imagines Lady Mason's guilt would have on his reputation: "It had been everything to him to be spoken of by the world as a man free from reproach,—who had lived with clean hands and with clean people around him" (2:195). The hero at the center of Peregrine's castle is a character in a narrative about purity and pollution, in which the latter projects a dread of social exclusion: given the choice between marriage to Lady Mason and the preservation of his spotless status in the minds of others, he can only choose the latter.

But the novel's chief castle-builder is Lady Mason herself, whose twenty-year occupation of Orley Farm is the result of her own fabrication: the forgery of a signature to her husband's will. Like Furnival, Lady Mason is invested not in a structure she believes to be true but rather in one whose reality and, crucially, legitimacy she works to frame as acceptable in the minds of others. The essence of her story is the confrontation between her initial fantasy of securing the property for her son and the twenty-years' labor involved in keeping that fantasy afloat: the continual friction between the structure she has built and the effort it takes to maintain it. According to the law, she has committed a crime. And yet she too is, like Furnival, Peregrine, and Trollope himself, a castle-builder, with the crucial difference that she did indeed act on impulse one fateful night. Having done so, she has since learned the lesson that she must subject every subsequent action to meticulous strategizing: she cannot make the smallest move without a detailed consideration of its possible public reverberations. And crucially, as he does for Furnival and Peregrine, Trollope constructs her castle-building as a characteristic and habitual activity.

The novel frequently calls attention to Lady Mason's internal debates. Her thinking is a private activity: she often does it alone, in a room, behind closed doors. ("She knew that her enemies were conspiring against her,—against her and against her son; and what steps might she best take in order that she might baffle them?" [I:46]) She muses about her need to secure Peregrine's support and the question of whether to put herself in Furnival's hands at once (I:48); she considers how to behave with her son, given that he will hear rumors about her ("Difficult as the task would be to her, it would be best that she should prepare him. So she sat alone until dinner-time planning how she should do this. She had sat alone for hours in the same way planning how she would tell her story to Sir Peregrine; and again as to her second story to Mr. Furnival" [I:149]). Throughout, the novel carefully notes the amount of time her thinking takes, its material surroundings, and, as she herself does, the difference between her private self and the self she displays in public: "Once or twice she rubbed her hands across her forehead, brushing back her hair, and showing, had there been anyone by to see it, that there was many a gray lock mixed in with the brown hairs. Had there been anyone by, she would have been more careful" (I:46). Having one dark night committed the act that, we are frequently told, defines the rest of her life ("She had striven to be true and honest,—true and honest with the exception of that one deed. But that one deed had communicated its poison to her whole life" [2:233].)—she spends the next twenty years managing her internal and external condition, cautiously observing her effect on others. And for this reflection and the self-composition that accompanies it—the careful management of her outward demeanor so as to manage the thoughts of others—Trollope uses the term "labor":

> But the absolute bodily labour which she was forced to endure was so hard upon her! She would dress herself, and smooth her brow for the trial; but that dressing herself, and that maintenance of a smooth brow would impose upon her an amount of toil which would almost overtask her physical strength. . . . She longed for rest,—to be able to lay aside the terrible fatigue of being ever on the watch. From the burden of that necessity she had never been free since her crime had first been committed. (2:232)

Like Sir Peregrine and Felix Graham, the cogitating Lady Mason is pictured in a manner that literalizes the constraints, both material and immaterial, that have arisen around her fantasy and its necessary maintenance; unlike her author, having neglected realist constraints she cannot lay her identity aside. And so her labor continues: here, for instance, she sits in a room in Sir Peregrine's home ("a small breakfast parlour, which was used every morning, but which was rarely visited afterwards during the day") while he consults with Furnival:

> Here she sat, leaving the door slightly open, so that she might know when Mr. Furnival left the baronet. Here she sat for a full hour, waiting—waiting—waiting. There was no sofa or lounging-chair in the room, reclining in which she could remain there half sleeping, sitting comfortably at her ease; but she placed herself near the table, and leaning there with her face upon her hand, she waited patiently till Mr. Furnival had gone. That her mind was full of thoughts I need hardly say, but yet the hour seemed very long to her. (I:265)

What the narrator "need hardly say" encompasses a great deal here: if it is hardly necessary to report that Lady Mason is thinking, still less necessary is it, it appears, to detail the content of her thoughts. It is necessary, however, to report that a great deal of time is devoted to thinking and to elaborate what that thinking looks like. And those details tell us something we also know about Furnival, Peregrine, and Graham: these characters are thinking purposefully. The things described in these scenes—the bodily postures; the rooms; the bed, chairs, or absence thereof—refer both to the constraints of realist representation (displaying the work of the realist, bound to his genre) and to the larger context in which fantasy is enabled by the same social and economic structures that constrain or bind it. In this sense, the fantasy of owning Orley Farm that, for Lady Mason, renders its possession a prison is merely another version of the fantasy of reputation Peregrine has constructed for himself; the recursive loop of strategizing that endlessly occupies Furnival; the position as dependent friend Graham occupies in his friend's borrowed bedroom. The untasted biscuit and wine; Furnival's domestic difficulties, resulting especially in the disruption of dinners and teas; the constrained pleasures of the sickroom—such details suggest the way in which the creature comforts won in *Orley Farm* prove no more comforting, and no more settled, than those of the illicitly occupied Orley Farm.

Imagining thinking as a kind of labor, Trollope gives these characters the task of adjudicating at length the instabilities of their social and emotional positions: possessing the time, the privacy, and the surrounding structures (libraries, breakfast rooms, a bedroom provided by a wealthy friend) within which to do so, these characters incorporate castle-building into their identities and the structure of their days. And if the accoutrements of a Sir Peregrine or a Lady Mason might be the stuff of fantasy for some of Trollope's middle-class readers, the representation of that thinking as a kind of labor helps to bridge the distance: like the reading of serial fiction, thinking in this novel is imagined as a regular material practice, dedicated to a specific task. Indeed, it ties together leisure and labor in a manner reminiscent of the realist fantasy Trollope himself embodied, combining the pleasures of fox-hunting and club-going with a regular work-regimen, the former (fantasy) rendered possible by the realist approach of the latter (real). Dealing with a specific issue or problem; sitting in a specific place to do it, and doing it periodically and for an extended period of time, Trollope's characters engage in an activity that echoes their author's own aspirational endeavor. Representing thinking in this manner, he figures leisure as a kind of labor: what one needs to do to get ahead. And he figures it, moreover, as an activity whose rewards are superior to what the novels represent as the pleasurable but ultimately useless wish-fulfillments of the genre whose presence as an alternative mode they often invoke: sensation fiction.

For the building of castles in the air is not limited to the author and his characters: the novels' more extensive project is to teach readers to do the same. To some extent this project is advanced by a widely-noticed Trollopian device: the refusal of the kind of suspenseful withholding of detail associated with sensation fiction, often accompanied by a narratorial defense when a novel gives away plot details at a moment other novelists (and readers as well) might, the narrator suggests, see as premature. *Orley Farm* makes readers aware of Lady Mason's guilt almost from the beginning, something Trollope later said he regretted (*Autobiography* 167), but the doing of which nevertheless warns readers away from imagining that the gradual revelation of plot details could possibly be the novel's chief concern. "Our doctrine is," *Barchester Towers* famously informs us, "that the author and reader should move along together in full confidence with each other" (127). *Dr. Wortle's School* makes much the same point:

> There is a mystery respecting Mr. and Mrs. Peacocke which, according to all laws recognized in such matters, ought not to be elucidated till, let us say, the last chapter but two, so that your interest should be maintained almost to the end. . . . It is my purpose to disclose the mystery at once, and to ask you to look for your interest,—should you choose to go on with my chronicle,— simply in the conduct of my persons, during this disclosure, to others. . . . It may be that when I shall have once told the mystery there will no longer be any reason for interest in the tale to you. That there are many such readers of novels I know.[20]

Whether such passages constitute an accurate description of Trollopian practice is a subject of some dispute; several critics have suggested that such comments are "red herrings," and that Trollope's novels are sensational despite these caveats.[21] But accurate description is not the point of such passages: rather, they craftily construct a straw reader—a creature of desire—for whom the reading of any non-sensational fiction might prove too laborious a task. Interpellating his readers as superior to the "many" who prefer the pleasures of suspense, Trollope elevates the process of ratiocination and castle-building I have described: only a lesser kind of reader, he suggests, succumbs to a lesser kind of desire. And it is not just this kind of commentary that structures the reader's experience, but also the presence and representation of thinking itself: what readers are offered instead of sensation fiction, as an alternative to its rapid action, or as a supplement to it even in those instances when (as Jenny Bourne Taylor argues is the case in Trollope's novels) the action we get might in fact be deemed sensational. The reader of Trollope, the narrator asserts, must be a more patient, deliberate sort of reader; he or she must learn to substitute one form of reading, or thinking, for another, and that substitution involves learning to build castles in the air. It is not to the secrets of plot, but rather, as the passage from *Dr. Wortle's School* asserts, to "the conduct of my persons, during this disclosure, to others" that a reader should "look for your interest."

For the reader of Trollope, in contrast to the reader of sensation fiction, has work to do. On numerous occasions, for instance, *Orley Farm's* narrator seems just as uncertain of the facts as any reader might be. What can one say of Madeline Staveley? "Of her actual thoughts and deeds up to this period it is not necessary for our purposes that anything should be told; but of that which she might probably think or might possibly do, a fair guess may, I hope, be made from that which has been already written" (I:185–86). Or, of Mr. Furnival, "I cannot say why he obtained no great success till he was nearly fifty than forty years of age. . . . What was the special case by which Mr. Furnival obtained his great success no man could say. In all probability there was no special case. . . . Legal gentlemen are, I believe, quite as often bought off as bought up" (I:95). The reader whose image the novel projects has been schooled in the shortcomings of the law, and is well aware of the unlikelihood of any means of coming to a true solution, or resolution, through its mechanisms. Lady Mason, we are told, has "grown upon" the narrator during the course of the novel's writing so that he now regards her as a friend, though she has done wrong—but she has done wrong only in thinking of securing the property for her son. These are the thoughts with which the novel "bids farewell" to her (2:404), and their twists and turns, the possibility of feeling one way or another about her and about the case, remain. Providing a more complex view of Lady Mason than the simple polarization of "pure" and "stained," or the court's verdict, can encompass—offering us several official public views, and his own private one, to consider as well—Trollope advances the cause of his own realism by promoting the idea that characters and readers are best off judging for themselves: an activity in which an adherence to conventional constraints and proprieties (those of the law or of conventional morality) gives way to more complex, individuated reasoning about why she should not, or perhaps, given the circumstances, why she should, and, in any event, why we might like her or not like her nevertheless.

Having habituated us to the nature, the prominence, and perhaps above all the necessity of castle-building, the novel fashions its ideal reader as someone whose ability to see through the fantasies of stability such structures seem to provide leads to the essence of the Trollopian real. The reader thus taught will not merely obey prohibitions or require overt constraints in order to behave properly, but will instead arrive—or attempt to arrive—at his or her own conclusions. Such a reader might, in fact, resemble Lady Mason, who, found innocent by the court and hence free to keep the property she has fraudulently obtained, decides nevertheless to give it up.

For no one is in charge, in the end, but us (as Mr. Harding says toward the end of *The Warden*, "I have very little but an inward and an unguided conviction of my own to bring me to this step" [253])—and since as readers we have been taught to think by Trollope, we know what we must do: the precise content of our thinking need not be specified. The figure mirrored by the text's descriptions and actively created by its withholdings—that of a man or woman in a room, thinking—is one for whom the process of reading involves a detailed consideration of the probabilities, possibilities, and constraints that structure, and for Trollope produce, the real.

Chapter 4

"Outside the Gates of Everything"
Hardy's Exclusionary Realism

Space is never empty: it always embodies a meaning. The perception of gaps itself brings the whole body into play.

> Henri Lefebvre, *The Production of Space*

There can be no realism unless the reader simultaneously sees the glass and pretends that he does not see it.

> Walter Kendrick, *The Novel-Machine:*
> *The Theory and Fiction of Anthony Trollope*

Windows: You can see what's outside yet feel safe and protected. It's all thanks to windows. Who thought up windows? We may never know. But that man or lady had it "goin' on!"

> Jack Pendarvis, "The Fifty Greatest Things That Just Popped
> into My Head"; *The Believer Magazine*

For the present he was outside the gates of everything, colleges included; perhaps some day he would be inside.

> Thomas Hardy, Jude the Obscure

Toward the end of Thomas Hardy's *The Return of the Native*, Clym Yeobright—having lost his wife Eustacia to drowning; survived the entanglement in the river that kills his rival Wildeve; and effectively lost a second wife in the marriage of his cousin Thomasin to Diggory Venn—stands with the boy Charley outside the window of the house at Blooms-End in which Thomasin and Venn are celebrating their wedding. He appeals to Charley for help making out the scene, since, as he puts it, his sight is weak and the glass is not good. He does not want a disinterested account of what's there, however, but has something already in mind: Clym seeks in this picture some indication that the festivities refer, in some way, to him.

"Do any of them seem to care about my not being there?" Clym asked.
"No—not a bit in the world. Now they are all holding up their glasses and drinking someone's health."
"I wonder if it is mine?"
"No—'tis Mr. and Mrs. Venn's."[1]

What would it look like, one wonders, if they did care? How would a toast to Clym look different from a toast to someone else? What exactly is it that Clym imagines would be described to him? (And why, after the first answer, does he persist, going on to ask again?)

Later that evening, after the newlyweds have left, Clym "sat down in one of the vacant chairs opposite his mother's old chair," which "had been sat in that evening by those who scarcely remembered that it ever was hers."

> But to Clym she was almost a presence there, now as always. Whatever she was in other people's memories, in his she was the sublime saint whose radiance even his tenderness for Eustacia could not obscure. But his heart was heavy: that mother had not crowned him in the day of his espousals. . . . And events had borne out the accuracy of her judgment, and proved the devotedness of her care. . . . He should have heeded her, for Eustacia's sake more than for his own. (388)

"Events had borne out the accuracy of her judgment, and proved the devotedness of her care." If, in Hardy's novels—most famously this one—it is often difficult to distinguish background from foreground, characters from the landscapes they inhabit, these passages suggest a further concern in the realm of perception with a relationship between accuracy and care. If the first scene, viewed clearly, reveals an absence of care (somehow Charley knows what that absence looks like), the second imagines an accuracy guaranteed by care, in which the one who knows what's best for you is the one who sees through a caring lens: someone whose eyes project into any scene an awareness of a particular person's presence, every landscape providing an opportunity to raise a meta-phorical toast to that same person.

Keeping company with the presence of an absent mother might seem to follow naturally upon the discovery that the empty space one wishes to find at the center of the party is visible to no one but oneself. Indeed, maintaining as "presence, now and always" someone who is remembered chiefly for having kept you in mind suggests the one-way nature of the reflection Clym sets up here, in which the other—in this case, the mother—is remembered chiefly for the value of her percep-tion of the son: as the person who, with the peculiar accuracy bestowed by care, saw him best. Having lost, effectively, those who cared for him most—those to whom his continued existence would make the most difference—Clym peers sightlessly, hopefully, and against all odds for some indication that this picture (an example of what I want to call, in this argument, the novel's landscape) might still, unaccountably, be about him.

A similar constellation of concerns—tying issues of perception to the observer's status in the minds of others—occurs in *Jude the Obscure*:

> For many days he haunted the cloisters and quadrangles of the colleges at odd minutes in passing them . . . . The Christminster 'sentiment,' as it had been called, ate further and further into him; till he probably knew more about those buildings materially, artis-tically and historically, than any one of their inmates.
>
> It was not till now, when he found himself actually on the spot of his enthusiasm, that Jude perceived how far away from the object of that enthusiasm he really was. Only a wall divided him from those happy young contemporaries of his with whom he shared a common mental life. . . . Only a wall—but what a wall! . . . He was as far away from them as if he had been at the antipodes. . . . He was a young workman in a white blouse, and with stone-dust

in the creases of his clothes; and in passing him they did not even
see him, or hear him, rather saw through him as through a pane of
glass at their familiars beyond. Whatever they were to him, he to
them was not on the spot at all; and yet he had fancied he would be
close to their lives by coming there.

But the future lay ahead after all. . . . For the present he was
outside the gates of everything, colleges included; perhaps some
day he would be inside. Those palaces of light and learning; he
might some day look down on the world through their panes. . . .

From his window he could perceive the spire of the cathedral,
and the ogee dome under which resounded the great bell of the
city. The tall tower, tall belfry windows, and tall pinnacles of the
college by the bridge he could also get a glimpse of by going to the
staircase. These objects he used as stimulants when his faith in the
future was dim.[2]

"Only a wall divided him . . . but what a wall!" The stimulating action
of the architectural configurations Jude perceives, drawing him in their
direction, is countered by their inhabitants' general refusal to acknowledge him once he gets there: "they did not even see him, or hear him,
rather saw through him as through a pane of glass at their familiars
beyond." The wall that separates Jude from his contemporaries turns
out to be Jude himself: like Clym, he is invisible to those with whom he
is actually "on the spot"—a construction that, as in Clym's case, rather
than pointing toward something concealed marks a social and emotional invisibility, the suggestion that he is not, in fact, "on the spot" at
all. Here as elsewhere in Hardy's work, the construction of Wessex as
an abstraction, a series of boundary markers and place names, encounters another kind of construction, in which space and vision are infused
with subjectivity: every "spot" possessing a capacity either to acknowledge the subject or refuse to acknowledge him. That second kind of
map might, for instance, resemble the landscape of memory described
by Edard Fitzpiers, in *The Woodlanders,* as involving an "almost exhaus-
tive biographical or historical acquaintance with every object, animate
and inanimate, within the observer's horizon" (125); it might depict an

image of the heath on which Clym's eyes "had first opened" (171), which "hardly anybody could look upon . . . without thinking of him" (166).[3]

These scenes tie issues of visual perception (the possibility of seeing clearly; of conjuring a presence from an absence) to a psychological or affective focus on the self (whether some interest in the observer is manifest in the scene observed) in a manner that could be used to complicate the debate over Hardy's realism.[4] But the changes that these scenes, and others discussed below, wreak on realist conventions point, more saliently, toward a rereading of the conventions themselves: especially of the relation they construe between characters and physical spaces and places. For in these scenes Hardy complicates assumptions about realism's specularity—the space it constructs for its subjects through the evocation of visual signs—by calling attention to what I want to describe as realism's exclusionary potential.

Those rhetorical forms and metaphorical constructions most closely associated with realist representation, such as Althusserian interpellation, Albertian perspective, and metonymy—along with the devices that do their work, such as mirrors and windows—"hail" the subject, returning his image, assuring him of his centrality and coherence. But they also possess the potential for what might be called negative interpellation: the potential, that is, to keep him out. The realist landscape, knowing how to give the subject (or native) what he wants (the return of his image), also knows how to refuse it.[5] My concern is not that such refusals expose the subject's lack of coherence, as a postmodern reading might suggest, but rather that an emphasis on exclusion articulates the "real"—that to which everyone presumably has access—as bounded: if your surroundings can keep you out, you were never more than provisionally in. That is, it defines realism as realist fantasy: as a space that in some way reflects the perceiving subject. This issue is particularly charged in the context of Hardy's Wessex, a construction that, "like" Dorset but emphatically not Dorset, simultaneously invites us (readers) in and excludes us, the novels making use of the conventions of realistic representation even as they evoke a highly subjective universe in which the rules that govern "real" places need not obtain.[6] Exploiting and indeed exploding realist conventions by drawing out their exclusionary potential; suggesting, in doing so, the fantasmatic dimension of the idea of inclusion (for in this context perhaps the most familiar realist convention, metonymy—reading character in the things that surround it—appears only slightly less delusional than Clym's idea that every toast must be a toast to him), Hardy reveals the mechanics of those representational norms that, in realist fiction and the world outside it, seem unobtrusively to bind characters and readers to the places they inhabit.

In Clym's case, for instance, the filminess of the glass; the difficulty of seeing; the anxiety about and apprehension that those behind the window might be unaware of the viewing subject's absence—all of these suggest a transformation of an Althusserian interpellation scene. Rather than "hail" or call out to the subject, that is, inviting him in, the image framed by this window refuses to recognize him—refuses, literally, to see him at all. And the way in which Clym's weak eyes mirror the condition of the glass suggests that his inability to see those behind the window finds its corollary, if not its cause, in their absence of care. What he sees with Charley's help is an absence of recognition: an absence of care expressed as an absence or retreat of visuality itself.[7]

Clym's episode of not seeing/not caring supports the idea of a memory-infused landscape, bringing to a conclusion what might be called the fantasy of the native's return: a scenario wherein this figure called the native could be said to seek, through the act of returning, to assure himself of his own nativeness—that tie between place and identity on which realist novels and the characters in them depend. The native's fantasy, that is—the fantasy the term "native" embodies—may inhere less in your desire to return to a specific place than in the idea that the place, in some fashion, wants you. This, indeed, effectively describes what, theorists argue, landscape already is: as Elizabeth Helsinger points out, landscape is always about the viewer. While Helsinger's argument is generally concerned with the representation of nationality—the way English rural scenes project images of Englishness—she begins more abstractly with the notion of enclosure or bounded space: the idea that landscape literalizes an unspoken but shared set of values, representing "the space and time in which individuals who do not know one another can imagine themselves to coexist" (18–19). Following the work of Richard Helgerson, she describes the way landscapes, repeating certain historically-specific structural conventions, come to supplement maps and verbal description as a means of representing national land. Landscape, she points out, is a "'centered' form of topographical representation . . . constituted on a principle of centering relative to a 'viewer' observing it"; landscapes always "point to their observers"; "they project the possibility of a subject while they refer to a portion of the land" (24). Landscape, in other words, "needs" a viewer, is incomplete—is, in effect, not landscape—without a viewer. My argument about Hardy's novels in this chapter thus resituates for external landscapes the claims I made for the spectacularity of *Adam Bede*'s interiors—their reflection of the interiorities of readers and characters—while describing once more the way realist conventions typically seen as effacing the subject in fact point toward his or her presence. What readers and characters read as invitation and prohibition—again, seen as aspects of the same structure—articulate the boundaries of realist conventions.

　　To say that landscape desires its subject is to see such conventions as Albertian perspective and metonymy not as facts about realist representation but rather as projective structures, expressing a subject's desire to affirm his presence in the external world and identifying realism with the successful—because invisible—achievement of that desire. Indeed, what I want, here, to call Hardy's landscapes—including social and built environments as well as natural ones—do not simply refuse this reflection, but tend to present as obstacles (or, as in Jude's case, "walls") those things, such as windows and mirrors, that more conventional strategies of realist representation might efface or transform into more conventional metaphors (*Middlemarch*'s pier-glass is a good example).[8] Thus even when Jude imagines himself as having arrived, the glass that marked his distance from his goal does not disappear; rather, he simply changes sides (seeing himself excluded, on the wrong side of the glass, he imagines himself at some future time looking "down on the world" through the panes of those "palaces" he would then inhabit). Defamiliarizing by literalizing some of realist representation's familiar metaphorical devices—invoking their material properties and thereby problematizing their metaphorical ones—Hardy rewrites them as blocking mechanisms: objects that refuse to reflect in conventional ways; that exclude rather than (or even as) they include; that fail to conform to conventional scenarios of transparency and transmissi-bility.[9] Moreover, teasing out and juxtaposing the material and meta-phorical properties of these objects and suggesting as well the confining structure of metonymy itself, Hardy revises the contours of the bour-geois domesticity these conventions help construct: the things we sur-round ourselves with and the comfortable familiarity of the metaphors we make of them. In a stark schematics of exclusion and discomfort—depicting spaces you wouldn't want to be inside, but wouldn't want to be outside either—he reveals the dependence of bourgeois norms on the frames through which we see them, exposing his and his characters' simultaneous estrangement from and attachment to a culture that relies on their invisibility. My point is not, then, that Hardy's work is "anti-real-ist" because, for instance, the perspectives of individual characters fail to agree with one another; the failure of "points of view" to agree in such cases hardly destabilizes—indeed, it reinforces—normative notions of the real.[10] Rather, I propose that Hardy's simultaneous use and exposure of the structure of realist conventions renders his texts simultaneously realist and non-realist, a dual effect I am calling realist fantasy. That is, when realist conventions become visible as perceptual structures, the exclusionary or prohibitive side of the familiar realist invitation to read-erly participation and seamless identification becomes visible as well.

When Clym asks whether the scene at which he gazes registers his absence, Hardy uncovers, by literalizing, some of realist representations' key conventions and assumptions. In the treatise *Della pittura* (1435), for instance, Leon Battista Alberti mapped out the painter's mathemati-cally-fixed perspective via the use of a metaphorical window, diagram-ming the relation between observer and painterly object in a manner that has since served as a model for describing the conventions of realist representation. Alberti's window constitutes the observer by situating him, precisely, at the projected reverse of a vanishing point: that point at which both landscape and subject become coherent, the reflected viewer occupying what is in effect a vacancy—a spot that might be occupied by any number of interchangeable subjects.

Alberti's model suggests that what is seen as if through a win-dow mirrors the subject: this is another way of saying that it "sees" the subject—just as, in the metonymic structures of the conventional realist novel, objects and places quietly and without attracting notice return to the subject his or her own image. Of course the subject returned, reflected, or projected in all these instances—the coherent subject of representational strategies such as metonymy and Albertian perspective—is a misrecognition, a vacancy or vanishing point with which a subject must identify in order to be "seen" or recognized. Thus if the landscape or things around the subject refuse to hail him, as is the case with Clym and his window scene, the point would be not that he does not exist, but rather that he does not exist for others: the landscape in which he wishes to see himself does not return his gaze.

Accounts of classic realism describe the genre as an effect of shared codes: just as Albertian perspective renders a scene coherent for a subject at a specific vanishing point, so too does metonymy rely on conventional understanding (of the nature of "things" and, as I shall discuss further, of space as well) to elicit readerly assent. Both create the perception of a shared reality based on codes, the means by which bourgeois culture defines the real; both are forms of ideological hailing. But Alberti's use of surfaces or screens suggests the way in which realist representation also divides the subject from what he or she views, the surface or screen serving both as material the viewer sees through and as a barrier or site for projection. As in Hawthorne's description of Trollope's realism, Alberti's structure enables us to see the glass and not see it at the same time. Given Althusser's definition of ideology as representing "the imaginary relationship of individuals to their real conditions of existence," realism's effect of transparency— the capacity of realist representation to appear unmediated—would be shared only by those who are situated, literally or figuratively, on the same side of the glass: who possess the same imaginary relation to the real. Indeed, given that analysis, those who share the same metonymic connotations, seeing the same things as real, might just as well be said, as in a formulation by Slavoj Žižek, to participate in a "shared fantasy."[11]

Alberti's reliance on distance, as well as his use of a translucent or transparent surface to help him visualize lines of sight from his eye to the scene before him, points—as does Hardy's evocation of the cloudiness of the glass, and, elsewhere, of the material properties of transparent objects—toward the exclusionary potential of conventional realist representations, and of a culture defined by its attachment to them. For if realist representation requires the construction of a view that earns general assent, that view is also a constrained one—requiring the assent of a particular group to the shared qualities of a landscape and a narrative of their relation to it. Glass in particular inhabits a liminal and contradictory space between visibility and invisibility, materiality and metaphor, its transparency and illusion of openness countered by its function as a barrier or wall: a contradiction embodied in the way a picture of fellowship, like the wedding at Blooms-End, includes within it both an invitation to participate and the impossibility of a particular viewer's participation.[12]

The classic realist text, writes Colin MacCabe, "cannot deal with the real as contradictory"; it "ensures the position of the subject in a relation of dominant specularity." "The relation between the reading subject and the real is placed as one of pure specularity. The real is not articulated—it is" (39). Writes John Roberts, "What is depicted is held—by producer and viewer alike—to be the result of an unmediated process, of transcription or recovery."[13] For the subject of classic realism, landscape ideally anchors or secures a position in the world; in particular, as in the example of Clym and his window, what viewers or subjects ask their landscapes to do—not just their natural environments, but their social ones as well (buildings and people)—is to include them: to affirm their identities as subjects.[14] Hardy disrupts the ostensibly placid specularity of classic realism not just by thwarting ambition, as in Jude's case (so that the place he wants to acknowledge him refuses to do so), but also by interrupting the recovery or return of the image, as in the example of Clym: literalizing as well as frustrating the assumption, foundational for realist fiction (and for the bourgeois subject, whose identity is tied to his possessions and environment) that characters will recognize a coherent self in their surroundings.

"The mind is not a thing of space," Jill Matus writes, citing Freud's critique of his own use of spatial metaphors for mental activity (311). But Hardy makes it one, as characters enter and exit spaces that seem to exist less as the houses they literally are than as metonymic extensions or symbolic representations of their own and other characters' heads.

Indeed, these houses hardly exist at all as domestic spaces, but rather limn stark demarcations between inside and outside: including some, excluding others, and staging dramatic scenarios about doing so. Near the beginning of *The Woodlanders*, for instance, Grace Melbury visits the physician Edred Fitzpiers, newly arrived in town, whom she has not yet met. Unaware that he is at home, she is admitted by a servant to wait for him, and enters his room to find him slumbering on a couch. Though, as Hardy puts it, the "windows of [his] soul were shuttered," a strange scene ensues: as Grace approaches the bell-pull to summon the servant, turning her back on Fitzpiers, she sees his image in a mirror. "An indescribable thrill passed through her as she perceived that the eyes of the projected image were open, gazing wonderingly at her." She turns to face him, only to discover that the man himself is still asleep.[15]

"In the reflection from the mirror which Grace had beheld there was no mystery; he had opened his eyes for a few moments, but had immediately relapsed into unconsciousness, if indeed he had ever been positively awake" (129). The episode leads Fitzpiers to imagine that he has dreamed of Grace, and leads Grace to wonder whether he has deceived her by pretending to be asleep. The rhetoric that separates the image of eyes on a reflected surface from the eyes in Fitzpiers's face also situates Fitzpiers and Grace on either side of a reality that has (at least) two sides: what she sees outside the mirror fails to coincide with what the mirror reflects. Later, when Fitzpiers awakens and Grace returns, the two exchange accounts, eventually constructing an episode susceptible to rational explanation; they come to terms, in other words, with an experience that seems inexplicably to situate them in different realities, and work to construct a shared reality out of it. And yet the passage retains the mysteriousness it hastens to explain away: the eyes were indeed "in the reflected image" rather than in the face being reflected.[16]

The detachment of eye from person makes vision a kind of floating property: the same kind that inheres in landscape, as Hardy himself projected in a drawing of his spectacles—a drawing in which vision, imagined as a function not of eyes but of lenses, shares many of the characteristics I have discussed here (fig. 1).[17] Surroundings that "reflect" character, that is, must in some way be imagined as looking at character—a phenomenon literalized by this scene's use of the mirror.

Figure 1. Thomas Hardy, "In a Eweleaze near Weatherbury (1898)." From *Wessex Poems and Other Verses*. London: Harper, 1903.

Viewing in the glass not her own image but rather that of Fitzpiers gazing at her (indeed, entering into a *mise-en-abyme* of reflected gazes, in which she might be imagined as seeing her reflection in the reflected eyes, and so on indefinitely), Grace sees a version of what Clym wants to see at Blooms-End: an image of herself "captured" (desired) by another's gaze. For despite her discomfort at being observed by the sleeping Fitzpiers, the "thrill" she experiences is that of being apprehended by the floating eye: the opposite of the affective emptiness left, for Clym, by Charley's answers in the scene discussed at the outset of this chapter.[18]

The mirror that reflects Fitzpiers's open eyes performs the same operation that defines Mrs. Yeobright's imagined focus on her son (the focus, that is, that Clym imagines). It reproduces and in doing so clarifies what I would argue Hardy exposes as realism's underlying dynamic: the projection of an imaginary realm in which the subject, in response to some prior perception or apprehension of exclusion, conjures up a gaze that wholly includes him or her—indeed, that holds him or her captive—in a manner that imprisons as much as it idealizes. In this scene, the narrator's "if indeed" leaves unanswered the question of whether the episode takes place solely within a character's mind: it leaves unresolved, that is—as does novelistic realism in general—the epistemological status of the real.[19] As in the ring of bonfires by means of which Egdon Heath's denizens locate one another in the darkness, a subject is seen—acknowledged—by light coming from (or bouncing off) another subject, as if the establishing of a shared reality requires the enlisting of another's belief in what might otherwise remain an isolated vision (while the image of ricocheting light suggests Žižek's shared fantasy). Just as Grace and Fitzpiers must come to an agreement about what happened in the mirror, so too does Clym reiterate his question to Charley: what he wants is nothing more than the boy's assent to his view of things.

Says Clym to Diggory Venn after Eustacia's death, "She is the second woman I have killed this year. I was a great cause of my mother's death, and I am the chief cause of hers."

"How?" said Venn.

"I spoke cruel words to her, and she left my house. I did not invite her back till it was too late. It is I who ought to have drowned myself. . . ."

"But you can't charge yourself with crimes in that way," said Venn. "You may as well say that the parents be the cause of a murder by the child, for without the parents the child would have never been begot." (361-62)

"You may as well say": the choice between realities in Hardy's fiction sometimes seems to come down to little more than this. What Clym wants to say—the reality he wants to assert, that he has caused his mother's death as well as Eustacia's—situates him at the story's center: a position he has for others long ceased to occupy, and one he occupies only, at this point in the narrative, in his own mind. But it was, of course, the position his mother maintained for him—and is the one he continues to maintain for himself by projecting his image in *her* head: the image, that is, of her insistent focus on him. Here she is, on her way back from Clym's and Eustacia's house, after the latter has refused to let her in (and Clym, sleeping, does not intervene):

Her eyes were fixed on the ground; within her two sights were graven; that of Clym's hook and brambles at the door, and that of a woman's face at a window. . . .

At length she reached a slope about two-thirds of the whole distance from Alderworth to her own home, where a little patch of shepherd's thyme intruded upon the path; and she sat down upon the perfumed mat it formed there. . . . She leant back to obtain more thorough rest, and the soft eastern portion of the sky was as great a relief to her eyes as the thyme was to her head. (275, 278)

"A woman's face at the window": the contest over Clym is defined by the vacant space this phrase leaves for its subject—a phrase that, like the window itself, looks two ways—as if the chief purpose of a window, or a house, is to mark a difference between the included and the excluded.[20] The image of the rejecting face behind the glass, along with the metonymic suggestion of Clym's presence and therefore implied assent to his mother's exclusion (his work-tools on the door) provides enough evidence for readers to assent to Clym's self-conviction, but only if we allow that his landscape embodies intentions of which he is unaware: that his house stages a closet psychodrama for him while he sleeps.[21] For the house, that quintessential Victorian realist enclosure, is here little more than a frame: a structure built to keep some ("a woman") in and others ("a woman") out. A social form (the house), reinforcing the structure of another social form (marriage), differentiates one woman (the wife) from another (the mother). Asleep while his mother is turned away, Clym too is both excluded—what happens is not his fault—and included: the scene is all about him. (Indeed, the passage ends with an image outside the realm not only of Clym's perception, but of his imagination: his mother's "relief" at the sight of vacant sky, devoid of the images with which she has been burdened.) Given the attenuation of agency encoded in this scene, in which social forms enforce what Clym does not (the window, the walls, the house, the marriage—all keep the mother out), Venn's remark is compelling: the parents may indeed be the cause of a murder that the child commits, just as the child may be the cause of his mother's death though he was asleep when she was turned away from the house.

Toward the end of *The Woodlanders*, Grace is fleeing Fitzpiers, now her husband, who has had an affair with Felice Charmond. Giles

Winterbourne, the man she loves but did not marry, offers to hide her for several days in what can only be called his primitive hut, until a time at which both believe she can safely make her way out of town. Observing what both consider the necessary proprieties, or what Grace calls "correctness," Giles remains outside, exposing himself to harsh weather. But he is closer than Grace suspects: kept near by illness, he lets her see him only in darkness and only through a window, so she cannot see how sick he is. Keeping Grace "safe," Giles also, of course, keeps her safe for himself, though this is not his acknowledged purpose; she is locked in presumably for her own protection, and remains indoors for fear of being noticed. Her activity is limited to waiting and preparing meals for herself and for Giles—meals she hands to him through a window. [22]

The Woodlanders is not a text in which characters easily share the same realities; indeed, they are most frequently aligned with one another by deceit or coercion. With a plot structured by a series of capturings and misrecognitions (Fitzpiers's initial fascination with Grace stems from his belief that she is Mrs. Charmond; his capturing of her image in the mirror reappears, in a different guise, in Giles's capture of her inside his hut) the novel is structured as a series of "man [or woman]-traps," a metaphor literalized at the end when Grace's dress is actually caught in the teeth of such a device.

The positioning of Giles and Grace in relation to the hut reshuffles, as dream-logic might do, the terms of Clym's nearsighted search for the empty space he imagines he might occupy at Blooms-End. This time, however, the image depicts not the absence of care but rather its opposite: something more like the picture Clym wished to see. In a staging of bourgeois domesticity like none other in Hardy, Grace is sequestered in the hut with nothing to do but wait: always on the lookout for Giles, and always with his breakfast or dinner waiting.

The only way to be sure the party is about you, one might conclude, is to have absolute control over who is in the house. *The Woodlanders*, writes John Goode, is a novel that "demolishes the social forms of relationship"; it is set, he also observes (quoting the novel) "outside the gates of the world."[23] Outside the gates of the world, it would seem, dinner is waiting; outside the gates of the world, indeed, hardly anything survives but "the social forms of relationship," especially those that might, were Giles willing to enter the house and Grace willing to let him, define them as the married couple they would, absent a few plot twists, have become. The two are sealed off from one another no more by the walls of the hut than by their observance of the invisible barrier that keeps them apart, a barrier they alone insist on maintaining (no one else is around to maintain it): the "correctness" that upholds a pretense of civilization in an otherwise wild and primitive scene. They cling to their walls, both real and metaphorical: Grace could walk out, but she does not; Giles could save himself by going indoors, but he does not. Indeed, the only reality they share is that of the boundary they refuse to cross— the fantasy that he is protecting her, from himself as well as others—as if the loss of structure entailed in crossing this boundary (opening doors as well as windows) would shatter their belief in what is most important to both: their mutual idealization ("There was one man on earth in whom she believed absolutely, and he was that man" [394]).[24] This scenario, identifying the conventions to which Giles and Grace adhere with the physical boundaries of walls and windows, articulates the barriers to which they cling as both inclusive and exclusive. The open window through which they communicate without being able to see one another distinctly is, in this scenario, no less a screen, simultaneously inviting and excluding, than the closed one at Blooms-End is for Clym; the mutually agreed-upon decision to respect the boundary of convention, here, perpetuates the pair's mutual idealization.

Indeed, this is not just a fantasy of bourgeois domesticity, nearly unrecognizable as such because of the strangeness of its context; it is also, on several levels, a fantasy about the exaltation of the excluded. Only "outside the gates of the world," for instance (only in Wessex?), after the central events of the narrative (marriage to the wrong person; deceit; adultery) have been concluded, can Giles and Grace have their relationship; only outside the gates of the world would someone think, as Giles apparently does, that exposure to the point of death is an appropriate price to pay for Grace's presence. Both Clym and Giles live "outside the gates of everything": outside the norms of bourgeois marriage, prohibited in Clym's case by Thomasin's choice of Venn and in Giles's by Grace's marriage to

Fitzpiers; outside the norms of realist fiction, in which no such bizarre scenario would be enacted. But here, outside the gates, the fantasy of exclusion is also, patently, one of inclusion, focusing attention on the character's attachment to that from which he is excluded (or, more precisely, in Giles's case, excludes himself)—as in Giles's and Grace's simulation of marriage. The narrative of exclusion is revealed to be what, of course, it always was—a narrative of centrality and martyrdom: in Clym's focus on his mother and his role as itinerant preacher; in Giles's extended suffering and then death, which leads Grace and Marty South to worship him. Exclusion becomes both reason for and evidence of elevation or singularity, and, finally, of inclusion in that most sequestered of imaginary spaces—that of another's mind—so that not being seen, or rather, being "seen" by those who cannot literally see one (the absent mother; the woman sequestered in the house) becomes a means, and perhaps the only means, of being seen best. To paraphrase Fitzpiers's remark, not only is what one loves inside one's head but it is also, fantasmatically, in someone else's—as in the image Clym projects from his mother's vacant chair, or the multiply reflecting images of Fitzpiers and Grace. [25]

What does it mean to say, as Clym says of his mother, that "events had borne out the accuracy of her judgment"? "Events" in Hardy famously "bear out," but the meaning of their doing so is never clear. Missed meetings, missed letters, bad weather: "events" construct a narrative that is simultaneously no one's fault and everyone's, punishing someone in particular despite the fact that no one in particular can be said unequivocally to deserve such punishment. The structure of causality enacted in much of Hardy's fiction might be said to raise "You may as well say" to a narrative principle: why not have things turn out this way; who can say they would not?[26] What, if anything, anchors "events" in anything more than individual fantasy?

When Clym returns to Egdon Heath, he appreciates his native land in a conventional way, as landscape: "He gazed upon the wide prospect as he walked, and was glad"—viewing the same scenery that, the narrative asserts, "hardly anybody could look upon . . . without thinking of him" (170–71). Mrs. Yeobright's focus on Clym is, in effect, universalized: the landscape "hardly anybody could look upon . . . without

thinking of him" *is* Egdon Heath, not someone's idea of it. Accuracy
meshes with care to produce what almost everyone perceives, the novel's opening implicitly endorsing the mother's view: projecting a Clym-
centered landscape without apparent boundaries or frames.[27]
But as Clym moves away from his mother and toward Eustacia—
as he gives up the perception of himself that fit so seamlessly with his
own—("their [his and his mother's] discourses [were] as if carried on
between the right and the left hands of the same body" [185])—the
nature of his "nativeness" shifts as well: from the possibility of a mutual
appreciation of landscape to an isolated and isolating closeness, a perception too limited, too narrowly defined, to be shared. Eventually, this
is his condition:

> His daily life was of a curious microscopic sort, his whole world
> being limited to a circuit of a few feet from his person. His famil-
> iars were creeping and winged things, and they seemed to enroll
> him in their band. . . . The strange amber-coloured butterflies
> which Egdon produced, and which were never seen elsewhere,
> quivered in the breath of his lips, alighted upon his bowed back,
> and sported with the glittering point of his hook as he flourished
> it up and down. (244)

The comfortable, "normal" distance that had defined Clym's landscape
as one in which almost everyone sees him becomes uncomfortably and
unrecognizably narrow, the emphasis shifting from the nature of his
surroundings to the closeness of their attachment to him. Indeed, Clym
comes to be defined less by the nature of the things that surround him
than by their proximity to him, a transformation that calls attention to
metonymy's dependence on normalized spatial relations: the usually
invisible, because taken-for-granted, structuring of the self's relation to
its surroundings.[28] His identity narrows to match the limitations of his
vision, so that there is, literally, no room for anyone else in his personal
landscape (suggesting that you can only be the center of your own narrative if everything that, and everyone who, would interfere with that
centrality has been removed); his surroundings, rather than reflect him,

literally "stick" to him (as Venn the reddleman's work material sticks to him). The unusual closeness of Clym's environment draws attention away from a conventional understanding of the way metonymy in realist fiction works—that character may be understood via our conventional knowledge of the things that surround it—and toward the assumptions on which this kind of reading depends: that objects and surroundings exist "for" the subject (as in Jude's use of Chistminster's spires as "stimulants" for his imagination).[29]

Metonymy, of course, suggests a necessary connection between character (or person) and place; the mind, metonymy tells us, is a thing of space. But metonymy also, Hardy shows, defines the boundary between the native and the non-native—not just in this novel, but in any discourse in which characters are tied to place, most obviously in accounts of the sentimental power of a "native" or "home" land. Shrinking the boundaries of Clym's landscape, the novel calls attention to—by estranging us from—the normalization of spatial relations on which shared realist representation depends: the way in which, as in Helsinger's analysis or Albertian perspective, landscape, in order to be shared (in order to be landscape) must make room not just for a single viewer but for any number of viewers. In the increasingly exclusive nature of Clym's vision, as in Jude's less exclusive but similarly self-centered one, nativeness appears as what it less transparently is elsewhere: a defining and narrowing of boundaries.[30] For in calling attention to the way metonymy's structure encloses its subject, Clym's atmosphere calls attention as well to the way the more spacious landscape of the novel's opening—the "prospect" of the heath—is similarly bounded: not by a difference between subjectivity and objectivity (the landscape of memory versus a more "objectively" defined landscape), but rather by the inherently exclusionary nature of realist representation. Thus if one's native soil exerts, as the soil of Egdon Heath is said to do, a kind of magnetic attraction for those who belong to it, then the idea of the native's return signals not just Clym's personal journey, but also the nature of his, and perhaps any character's or person's, metonymic connection to his or her "native" place or home. Clym is *the* native—the only member of the club to which he belongs—not just because he comes back, as anyone might, but because nativeness itself, the quality of belonging to a particular place, is with particular emphasis embodied in him.

J.H. Miller calls Hardy's use of natural landscape "a complex form of metonymy whereby environment may be a figure for . . . the agents who move, act, and interact with the scene. . . . Perhaps this can work so unostentatiously because we readers of novels live our own lives in the material world that way" (20). In "typical" metonymic readings of realist fiction, Elaine Freedgood argues, "the object (as in metaphor) is indentured to the subject: a character's possessions, for example, if they are mentioned with a certain degree of emphasis, are meant to tell us something about that character and not about themselves or their own social lives. . . . Metonymy . . . tends toward the conventional, the obvious, the literal, the material—it often conjures up the real so successfully that its status as a trope seems to disappear" (*Ideas* 12). Rather than subordinate metonymy to the subject or to the realist novel, however, we might emphasize its function as the figure that most effectively renders the assimilation of modern identity to material things and surroundings, precisely, unostentatious, helping us take for granted that surroundings and possessions do indeed refer to and define identities. Instead of defining metonymy as the rhetorical technique that predominates in realist fiction, that is, we might see realist fiction (or any form of realist narrative, such as cinema) as the form that shores up metonymy, supporting a world view in which an individual is defined by and sees himself reflected in his things and surroundings. Metonymy, in other words, finds its imaginative justification and fantasmatic form in the realist novel.

Mrs. Yeobright, as Clym puts it, is always right. ("Strangely enough he began to feel now that it would not be so hard to persuade her who was his best friend that comparative poverty was essentially the higher course for him, as to reconcile to his feelings the act of persuading her. From every provident point of view his mother was so undoubtedly right, that he was not without a sickness of heart in finding he could shake her" [186].) The accuracy of her predictions is not, as we have seen, a function of objectivity but rather of its opposite; that is, it is marked not by the absence of a frame but by the invisibility of one.

> The love between the young man and his mother was strangely invisible now. Of love it may be said, the less earthly, the less demonstrative. In its absolutely indestructible form it reaches a profundity in which all exhibition of itself is painful. It was so with these. . . . Indeed, how could it be otherwise when he was a part of her, when their discourses were as if carried on between the right and left hands of the same body? (185)

The assertion of a connection between accuracy and care suggests that there is something neutral, inevitable—"real"—about events that confirm a particular affective judgment: his mother, Clym has told us, is always right. But if the accuracy guaranteed by care is guaranteed by the novel's fulfillment—she knew things would turn out this way—that fulfillment is also exposed as the making real or bringing to fruition of a particular fantasy (of, indeed, the fantasy of metonymy or nativeness itself, in which one's surroundings unproblematically reflect one's presence, or care about one); it is a scenario from which the frame that would reveal it as such has been effaced. The novel's ending (like its beginning, and like nativeness) situates readers (as it does Clym) in the realm of desire: in this case, a specifically maternal desire, in which what is left after the daughter-in-law and her partner in betrayal have been killed is the son's unending mourning of the mother—she who has, not least because of her own death, been proven right. The term "accuracy" removes the boundaries and frames (the pane of glass, the image of someone sleeping) that would expose this scenario as merely a choice among fantasies.

The realist novel is the form in which place mirrors the subject: the form that works to convince us not only that the mind is a thing of space, but that particular minds are reflected by and inextricably linked to—indeed, I have suggested, desired by—particular places and spaces. Hardy's demystification of metonymy anatomizes the connection between an imagined landscape and its inhabitants just as his attention to the blocking, exclusionary properties of objects that typically invite and reflect revises their relation to the "realism" of houses and homes. It is as if the invention of a new country, and significantly an imaginary one, requires a careful elaboration—a spelling-out—of the relation that obtains there between character and place, while that spelling-out also suggests an estrangement from the conventions that typically function more or less invisibly, in the realist novel, to offer us the "real." Wessex's estrangement from bourgeois norms is also an estrangement from the norms of realist representation—but not, of course, a disengagement from them. What Hardy once called the "partly real, partly dream-country" of Wessex lets us see the glass and pretend that we don't see it at the same time, dismantling the mechanisms that tie identity to place even as it represents, in Wessex and its characters, a connection so compelling that one can hardly help believing in it. [31]

Chapter 5

Armadale

Sensation Fiction Dreams of the Real

Wilkie Collins follows the single-volume edition of his sensation novel *Armadale* (1866) with an appendix that describes—with the somewhat impolitic addition of a gleeful exclamation point—the arrival in Liverpool of a ship on which three men have been found, victims of suffocation by poisoned air. Poisoned air, the novel's readers will recall, plays a significant role in the novel's denouement, while another incident involving suffocation on shipboard—a drowning in a locked cabin on a sinking ship—is a key element in the prehistory of its plot. Reports of the ship's arrival, Collins notes, followed publication of the novel's thirteenth number, and occurred one and a half years after "the end of the story . . . was first sketched in my note-book."[1] It is especially necessary to let readers know that his idea for the novel could not have been inspired by this particular bit of news, it would seem, because the name of the unfortunate ship, he announces—with the flourish of italics such a gift of unlooked-for coincidences undoubtedly deserves—is *The Armadale*.[2]

The appendix has two contradictory effects. On the one hand, it undercuts (or affects, tongue-in-cheek, to undercut) the novel's fantastical quality, insisting on the realist status of its bizarre foundation. On the other, it retrospectively transforms the novel into a predictor of actual events, aligning it with one of its central plot devices—the narrative called "Armadale's Dream"—whose fulfillment, revealing the identities of specific persons to fill the spaces of the dream's "shadows," forms the bulk of the novel's task.[3] Pointing out that one

of the novel's most extreme situations has occurred in actual life—
along with the additional, perhaps equally unaccountable detail that
the name "Armadale" exists in the real world—Collins simultaneously
gives his sensational novel a realist tweak and suggests the dreamlike
capacity of real-world events to fulfill and indeed encompass sensation fiction's wildest fantasies. Because of a coincidence of naming,
the world of external realities is given the role of fulfilling the dream
that the novel now appears to have been, even as events in the external
world, as attested to by a newspaper report, are summoned to affirm
the plausibility or realism of the novel's sensational beginnings. The
appendix brings the novel into view as a space of mediation between
fantasy, sensation fiction, and dream, on the one hand, and external
reality or the real on the other, even as it suggests the instability of
each term.[4]

One of the shrewdest analysts of *Armadale*'s complex structure,
Jenny Bourne Taylor, laments the novel's inability to "offer a stable
interpretation of itself to the reader" (171).[5] And indeed, in appealing
to the ostensibly inarguable status of the extra-novelistic real (despite
what might be said about the reliability of newspapers), Collins's gesture toward the real ship *Armadale* might be seen as an attempt to stabilize a narrative many readers have found incoherent and haphazard.
For one effect of the novel's abundant plot twists and turns is that it
seems to matter little at any given moment what direction its narrative
or characters take, just as it seems to matter little how many of them
are named "Armadale." When, for instance, Jeremy Bashwood tells his
father to "Fancy anything you like—there's nothing to stop you" while
recounting the story of Lydia Gwilt's background, he might as well be
referring to the structure of the novel as a whole. Like the novel's larger
framework, his narrative, Jeremy suggests, is flexible enough to tolerate
any number of possible alterations: "She may be the daughter of a Duke,
or the daughter of a costermonger. The circumstances may be highly
romantic, or utterly commonplace" (521). Indeed, *Armadale* seems less
structured by a coherent and necessary unfolding of specific events than
by the promise or threat of eventual repetition: the idea that the sins of
the fathers might be repeated by the sons bearing their name. And even

in this context the anticipation of such repetition is countered by the haphazard quality of individual moments: the "fancy anything you like" quality the narrative seems to possess.

What might rein in this apparent randomness, the appendix implies, is the real: an event posited as having actually happened, whether within the novel's framework or outside it, could serve as a kind of anchor, a limit or framework for subsequent events.[6] And yet in this case, the ostensibly stabilizing real not only acts as a provocation to fantasy but also resembles it: buried in layers of mediation so dense that it seems to recede into an illimitable and unrecoverable past, the novel's key event—the drowning, in a locked cabin on a sinking ship, of one Allan Armadale by another—and its subsequent echo call to mind what Slavoz Žižek has dubbed "a universal play of illusory mirroring," in which what we call reality and what we call dream are equally illusory versions of one another (*Sublime*, 48).[7]

Armadale's dream is situated as the novel's initiatory and inaugural event, despite the postponement of its appearance until the novel's fifth chapter. Transcribed by Armadale's friend Midwinter (originally named Allan Armadale), "Allan Armadale's Dream" appears as a series of numbered tableaux. It prominently features two indistinguishable "Shadows," the "Shadow of a Man" and the "Shadow of a Woman": outlines of figures whose identities, according to Midwinter's "supernatural" interpretation, will be revealed at some future time (though he already believes the "Man" to be himself). So designated, this portion of the text has naturally become the one that critics, like the novel's own dream-theorists Midwinter and Dr. Hawbury, have grappled with as dream, wondering along with the novel's characters and narrator how to interpret it, and considering especially whether, as an elaboration of the effects of the book's originary narrative—the murder of Midwinter's father by the elder Armadale—it determines the future of these characters, or whether they will be able to bypass its power and forge their own destinies.[8] And yet the setting aside of a narrative clearly marked as a dream deflects attention from the dreamlike quality of other events, most notably the drowning recounted at the novel's beginning and the attempted murder by suffocation at its end. Indeed, the first event—posited as the source or ground of all that follows—exists, like

Armadale's dream, in a *mise-en-abyme* of representation which destabilizes both its ontological status and its relation to the novelistic real. The drowning, in fact, resembles a primal scene, with all the ontological instability that term suggests. Like Armadale's dream, it appears only in highly mediated form. As the novel begins, the elder Armadale, on his deathbed, records in a letter to his son—to be read at some future time—the story of his own murder of a man known as Ingleby, actually Midwinter's father (both father and son are named Allan Armadale), by locking him in a cabin on a sinking ship. Like Armadale's dream, this narrative appears as a written text read aloud by someone who is not its author: in this case one Mr. Neal, a visitor said to be the only English speaker available for the task. And in a gesture that further attenuates the tale of the story's transmission, not only is Neal called upon to read aloud those parts of the document already completed, but he is also asked to fill in the missing parts himself by taking down the words that the elder Armadale, afflicted by paralysis, can no longer write. The scene is complicated, as well, by the positioning of Armadale's wife outside the door, where she hears the story her husband has hitherto kept secret from her.

The story of the murder is mediated not only by this complex record of relays from one person to another, but also by its numerous vague but suggestive mythic and Biblical resonances. The tale behind the murder of Allan Armadale II, calling himself Felix Ingleby, by Allan Wrentmore, calling himself Allan Armadale, is—like the story of its telling—complex and confusing; it is also a tale of theft, betrayal, mistaken identity, brotherly rivalry, and revenge. A prodigal son, Armadale, loses his inheritance when his father passes over him in favor of a nephew, Wrentmore, who then takes the Armadale name. The son takes revenge on the usurper—Wrentmore, now Armadale—by, as Ingleby, wooing and marrying Armadale's intended bride (with whom, in another mediated turn, he has fallen in love via a portrait enclosed in a letter sent by her father from Madeira. Armadale will have to travel there to claim his bride, whom he recognizes, upon arrival, as "the original of my portrait" [32]).[9] Ingleby, who had worked as a clerk for Armadale II, presents himself to the father, whose eyesight is failing (thus he cannot detect "Ingleby's" lack of resemblance to Wrentmore's mother); in a series of details reminiscent of the story of Jacob and Esau, "he [Ingleby] had learnt enough in my service to answer the few questions that were put to him" (33). If the plot of rival brothers has numerous literary and mythic echoes, the doubled names, desires, and family positions of the two men also give the murder something of the quality of the myth of Narcissus, whose attempt to merge with his reflected image results in his drowning.

Armadale's attempts to ground its narrative in or link it to the real, whether extra-or intra-novelistic, thus position any "original" scenes or encounters in a distant, heavily mediated past, even as the novel relies on them—and on the claim that, in the novel's universe of reported events, a specific incident is known to have occurred— as reference points or sources of stability for the winding, multi-layered narrative they ostensibly set in motion. The same holds true for the novel's use of dream theory, which proposes, like Freud's *Interpretation of Dreams* (whose publication follows that of Collins's novel by thirty-four years), that dreams draw their material from the mundane but undisputed facts of ordinary life.[10] After reading the narrative of Armadale's dream, one of the novel's doctors, Mr. Hawbury, declares (as Freud will soon after) that "A Dream is the reproduction, in the sleeping state of the brain, of images and impressions produced on it in the waking state; and this reproduction is more or less involved, imperfect, or contradictory, as the action of certain faculties in the dreamer is controlled more or less completely, by the influence of sleep" (137). For Freud too, a dream ("a little scene, a small story"; Žižek 45) is provoked by an irritant or stimulus from the dreamer's external context: "a stimulus coming from reality (the ringing of an alarm clock, knocking on the door . . . the smell of smoke)" (Žižek 44; see Freud 57). And indeed, dreams of drowning or suffocation may be prompted, Freud argues, by an external stimulus such as the slipping of a head beneath a pillow.

> If our bedclothes fall off in the night, we may dream, perhaps, of walking about naked or falling into water. If we are lying crosswise in bed and push our feet over the edge, we may dream that we are standing on the brink of a frightful precipice or that we are falling over a cliff. If our head happens to get under the pillow, we

dream of being beneath a huge overhanging rock which is on the point of burying us under its weight. (Freud 57; quoting Jessen [1855, 527 f.])

[T]he dreams of those suffering from diseases of the heart are usually short and come to a terrifying end at the moment of waking; their content almost always includes a situation involving a horrible death. Sufferers from diseases of the lungs dream of suffocation, crowding and fleeing . . . . Borner (1855) has succeeded in provoking the latter experimentally by lying on his face or covering the respiratory apertures. (68)

The narrative Armadale relates in his letter, and indeed the entire novel that follows it, might be reframed, according to this kind of interpretation (which the novel calls "rational" interpretation) as the response of a sleeping consciousness to an external stimulus.[11] Just as the arrival of the ship might be said, in the absence of (or despite) Collins's note defending against that possibility, to have retrospectively provoked Collins's novel, so too might the pillow's movement be said to give rise to the dream it seems to have stimulated. In other words, in an issue I shall return to below, even as the novel focuses on the question of whether a dream predicts or controls the future, the novel itself suggests in several ways that the present or future may predict or in fact create the past: that the past may be an effect of the future.[12]

All of the scenarios outlined above—Collins's gratification at the appearance of the ship named *Armadale*; the novel's positing of a scene that provides the impetus or rationale for all that follows; the idea, on which the novel relies, that dreams are grounded in the events of daily life—are aspects of what I want to call sensation fiction's dreaming of the real: the way in which this genre, positioned by both practitioners and critics in opposition to realism, gestures toward external realities and conventional realism, and indeed seems to require both as framework or anchor for its own claims and narrative effects. (Indeed, sensation fiction's desire for the real as well as for realism is best expressed in its self-professed claims to a more accurate realism than the conventional brand: its assertions that it exposes the unpleasant truths conventional realist novels dare not represent).[13] It is also the case that even as *Armadale* differentiates itself from realism as a genre, it requires and in the end seems to desire the ideological real—the world of accepted conventions—as in, for instance, the derided courtship of Armadale and Miss Milroy, or more generally the conventional behavior of men and women (discussed in more detail below). And there is yet another way in which this sensation novel dreams of the real, involving the particular nature of Armadale's dream.

Armadale dreams his dream, we are told, on board a French timber-ship called *La Grace de Dieu*, on the wreck of which he and Midwinter have temporarily been stranded (unbeknownst to both, this is the site of the murder of the father of one by the father of the other). He describes the narrative to Hawbury as "a much better account than I can give you," taken "all down in writing from my own lips"; "exactly what I dreamed, and exactly what I should have written down myself" (140–41). This emphasis on precision is belied by the material's heavily mediated quality: by its appearance as a written text, recorded by Midwinter and read aloud by Hawbury, as well as its rendering as a series of static images or tableaux numbered 1 through 17—a distinctly undreamlike, bullet-point organization.[14] The dream text is subject, moreover, not just to one interpretation but two: while Midwinter believes in a "supernatural" theory according to which the dream predicts future events, Hawbury interprets it according to his "rational" theory, in which the dream makes use of material from the external world.[15] The novel employs both interpretations, finding sources for the dream's images even as Armadale and Midwinter remain alert for its apparently predictive elements to be fulfilled, seeking in particular someone to fill the role of the "Woman Shadow"—a figure that appears in the dream at the edge of a pool and hands a glass of what appears to be poisoned liquid to a Shadow Man. The dream thus mediates and is mediated in several ways: it appears only as the result of a complex series of repetitions or reproductions, and it exists in a middle space between fantasy and the real, past and future, positionality and necessity—the latter referring to its structure as a narrative that offers positions or shadowy figures in place of specific persons, and more generally to the reliance on position that tends to characterize sensation fiction. Thus the gesture toward stability made by the novel's promise to fill those positions—to put unique identities in each place—is a key aspect of what I want to call this narrative's realist dream.[16] For in holding out the promise of unique persons who will occupy (or stabilize) its empty positions—specifically the positions designated for "A Man" and "A Woman"—*Armadale* aligns sensation fiction, as genre, with the dream at its center, both of them looking toward the moment when the variability and fungibility of sensational identity will be replaced the ostensibly singular characters of realist fiction.

> "The Names haunt me. I keep saying and saying to myself: Both alike!—Christian name and surname, both alike! A light-haired Allan Armadale, whom I have long since known of, and who is the son of my old mistress. A dark-haired Allan Armadale, whom I only know of now, and who is only known to others under the name of Ozias Midwinter. . . . So there are two of them—I can't help thinking of it—both unmarried. . . . And there are two Allan Armadales—two Allan Armadales—two Allan Armadales. There! Three is a lucky number. Haunt me again, after that, if you can!" (424).

Lydia Gwilt's drama, as she implicitly recognizes here—inspired as it is by the accident of encountering two Allan Armadales—is about positionality. The duplication of names renders possible the imagining of a sensational plot which ends with her possessing the body of one Allan and the wealth of the other, simultaneously doing away with and maintaining "Allan Armadale" in a series of moves that consolidate the two men into a single figure: the one who would have best suited her purposes all along. In what the proliferation of men with the same name renders a near-parody of sensation fiction's emphasis on position over person, *Armadale* invites consideration of the prominent role the sensation genre generally gives to position: its elevation of identity—name, lineage, property—over character; the important roles such devices as labels, name tags, and bits of material evidence play in pointing toward one character or another in novels such as *The Woman in White* and *Lady Audley's Secret*. This emphasis, as Ronald Thomas has so clearly pointed out, charts an ideological shift as well as a formal one, from a realist concern with character to a sensationalist preoccupation with identity.[17]

Žižek's brief discussion of dreams in *The Sublime Object of Ideology* refers to "the well-known paradox of Zhuang Zi, who dreamt of being a butterfly, and after his awakening posed himself a question: how does he know he is not *now* a butterfly dreaming of being Zhuang Zi?" The lesson Žižek, following Lacan, draws from this anecdote is that "the Lacanian definition of a fool is somebody who is not capable of a dialectically mediated identity with himself, like a king who thinks he is a king, who takes his being-a-king as his immediate property and not a symbolic mandate imposed on him by a network of intersubjective relations of which he is a part" (46). The alternative to wholly believing that you are a king, that is, is recognizing that the social forms that structure "our effective, real social relations" (Žižek 45) are themselves positions, ideological constructions distinct from and unallied with the persons who occupy them. The character I have discussed who makes this "realist" mistake— the king who thinks he really is a king—is *The Mayor of Casterbridge's* Michael Henchard, who is unable to perceive a difference between identity and role, especially in the case of the too-close affinity for or belief in his identity as Mayor. Seeing the Mayor as himself and himself as Mayor (just as Lucetta identifies with her effigy during the ride, saying "'Tis me" [275])—Henchard is unable to perceive the truth Hardy's title announces: that "Mayor of Casterbridge" designates not a person but a role, a symbolic mandate and title: a position capable of being filled by any number of individuals. Realism as a genre encourages this mistake—the illusory identification with the image—while sensation fiction tends to emphasize its opposite, focusing on the difference and distance between self and image, on impersonation and doublings of identity, the ease with which one person may be mistaken for another. Indeed, despite the ways in which realism has been said to acknowledge the fictitiousness of its own structures—perhaps even more because of this—it may be said to situate itself as the king of genres, emphasizing its awareness of the difference between the real and the not real even as it stresses the ineffable individuality of specific characters: the uniqueness of Dickens's Pip or Eliot's Dorothea Brooke.

Realism, then, like the realist character, might be said to believe what Žižek's fool does. The corollary of a character's belief in his or her self-identity or uniqueness would be a novel's belief, or the belief it wishes to compel, in its own representations—a belief, to borrow Žižek's phrase again, in its own illusory mirroring. What sensation fiction, with its dependence on impersonation, both knows and exposes, beyond such supposedly shocking facts as the prevalence in ordinary life of murder and bigamy, is the detachability of identities from roles or symbolic mandates. *Armadale* exploits this in the strangely non-referential quality of its title, which raises the question of reference both in the abundance of Armadales to which it points (a more accurate title for the novel might be *Armadales*) and its seeming refusal, as it proliferates Armadales, of the conventional purpose of naming itself (the distinguishing of one thing from another). What, or who, is an Armadale?—the novel's title seems to want us to ask. Maintaining an aura of impersonality by omitting a first name (which would identify the term as an individual's name, rather than, for instance, that of a town or a ship) the title recalls the ambiguity of *Villette* rather than the eponymous *David Copperfield* or *Jane Eyre*; it provokes the desire for a name, for the shape of an individual identity, by refusing to satisfy it, or by satisfying it halfway.[18] The word suggests singularity: it is, after all, an unusual name, and the title announces only one: *Armadale,* not *Armadales*. And yet of course there turn out to be several men claiming the name, which finally offers both more and less than bourgeois subjectivity ordinarily requires. The proliferation of Armadales points not, it turns out, toward singularity but rather toward positionality, not least because Lydia's plot literalizes the metaphor, depending on the substitution of the "light" Armadale for the "dark" one ("So there are two of them . . . both unmarried" [424]). So too does the survival of one Allan Armadale rest, at the novel's end, on logistics: the chance occupation of one room instead of another.[19]

If the dream points toward the positions that specific individuals will fill—that of the "Man-Shadow" and the "Woman-Shadow"—the novel suggests that the dream's fulfillment (the belief that "You, and no other" or "I, and no other" [564] must fill those positions) will offer the collapse of identity and position that, I have suggested, constitutes the error of realism as a genre. (This is the "it had to be you" I discussed in relation to *Oliver Twist*, in which the "anyone" Oliver might be overlaps with a determinist narrative in which his role can be filled only by his unique self). Collins, then, puts both sensation fiction and dream in the position of exposing the ideologies they promise to fulfill, and of fulfilling the ideologies they have worked to expose. The novel's characters in this reading become frameworks through which genre and ideology are refracted: mediators for ideologies that are dreaming of them.

Armadale is full of self-conscious allusions to the nature of men and women: discussions that restage the dream's casting-call for unique individuals to occupy the spaces it leaves unfilled. For instance: Armadale's lawyer Pedgift indulges in an extended discussion of the nature of woman, gleaned from his observations of witnesses.

> "When I was in the criminal branch of practice, it fell to my lot to take instructions for the defence of women committed for trial, from the womens' own lips. Whatever other difference there might be among them, I got, in time, to notice, among those who were particularly wicked and unquestionably guilty, one point in which they all resembled each other. Tall and short, old and young, handsome and ugly, they all had a secret self-possession that nothing could shake. On the surface they were as different as possible. Some of them were in a state of indignation; some of them were drowned in tears; some of them were full of pious confidence; and some of them were resolved to commit suicide before the night was out. But only put your finger suddenly on the weak point of the story told by any one of them, and there was an end of her rage, or her tears, or her piety, or her despair—and out came the genuine woman, in full possession of all her resources, with a neat little lie that exactly suited the circumstances of the case." (368)

The novel includes many other such remarks as well, about men as well as women. "The weak side of every man is the woman's side of him. We have only to discover the weak side of Mr. Armadale—to tickle him on it gently—and to lead him our way with a silken string" (609). "[T]he desperate concentration of strength of which women are capable in emergencies" (664). "Oh, the hardness of women to each other! Oh, the humiliation if men only knew some of us as we really are!" (386). "What fools women are!" (418). "He was in the mood in which trifles irritate a man, and fancies are all-powerful to exalt or depress his spirits" (390). "He spoke in a new voice—he suddenly commanded, as only men can" (422). "Are men as curious as women?" (383). Some of these are the narrator's observations; others are voiced by individual characters. In almost every example, the narrative of the position (man; woman) shares space with that of the individual undergoing the experience; individuality or perhaps just idiosyncracy seems to occupy a surface ("on the surface they were as different as possible") under which "genuine" character resides. All open up the same space the dream does for the position of "a man" or "a woman" to be filled by any individual belonging to the appropriate category, that is, and all expose a gendered ideology in which any man is interchangeable with any other, as is any woman.

Lydia Gwilt inhabits a sensationalist world of positionality: one in which, as she puts it, "I have been proved not to be myself" (283–84). Taking on a series of different identities during the course of the novel, including that of wife, Lydia embodies sensation fiction's characteristic reliance on identity's malleability and instability—an instability that depends on the elevation of the category or role over the idiosyncratic person, and on her skill in playing each part. "There are not many girls of twelve who could have imitated a man's handwriting, and held their tongues about it afterwards," she meditates, listing only one of her accomplishments (425). And yet the romance plot that develops between herself and Midwinter, oddly echoing and yet differentiating itself from the triviality and conventionality insisted upon between Armadale and Miss Milroy, points—like the dream—toward the resolution of indiscriminate positions in unique identities: the idea, as in all conventional romantic plots, that the occupant of a particular position must be a particular person: "You, and no other" (564).[20] The dream, like the love story, requires identity to be singular: not "the man" but Armadale, and even more specifically (in the unique opportunity this novel provides its lovers) not this Armadale but that one. "You, and no other, stood in the Woman's place at the pool. I, and no other, stood in the Man's place at the window. And you and I together, when the last Vision showed the Shadows together, stand in the Man's place and the Woman's place still!" (564). Midwinter's declaration bears on his own and Lydia Gwilt's fulfillment of the dream's prediction: the notion that despite his conscious intentions or actions, the two of them embody the fulfillment of Armadale's dream. If the novel's numerous other uses of the terms "the man" and "the woman" point toward the generic significance of these positions—the way specific persons or identities fulfill ideological positions—Lydia and Midwinter counter this belief with their own love story, realizing in their own imaginations specific figures who fulfill positions in an individual dream.

> An ideology is really "holding us" only when we do not feel any opposition between it and reality—that is, when the ideology succeeds in determining the mode of our everyday experience of reality itself.
>
> Žižek, *Sublime*, 49.

Realist ideology requires characters to identify with their particular roles—to believe that there is a unique place or position for their specific selves: "You, and no other"; "I, and no other." It requires, and revolves around, the mystery of unique identity, which Collins's fiction slyly refers to as the job taken on by the less-than-trustworthy to "preserve the characters to which we have committed ourselves" (634). But both *Armadale* and the dream at its center highlight the subject's generic and ideological nature: the Man-Shadow and Woman-Shadow; the man, the woman. As if protecting the realist notion of singular identity, the novel makes its two central Armadales, despite their shared name and linked ancestry, as different as possible in person, manner, sensibility, and complexion; as if to reassure readers, sameness and interchangeability are relegated to the novel's dark subplot—as, indeed, they are in many sensation novels. And even as they seem to oppose one another, and as the novel oscillates between them as generic choices, the story of uniqueness and the story of interchangeability may be also be said to mirror one another, just as realism and sensation fiction may be said to offer alternate but often mutually reinforcing perspectives on bourgeois ideology. But Collins offers another way of thinking about genre in *Armadale*'s emphasis on layers of transmissibility or mediation. For in the narrative's unexplained insistence (as Bourne Taylor remarks, the absence of a stable account of itself) on the passing of stories or texts from one character to another, as in its "rational" interpretation of dreams, a character or person becomes readable as a site where mediation takes place. As in Freud's articulation of the way dreams come into being, the body becomes a medium and mediator: a framework for the transformation of realist detail into sensationalist nightmare.

Late in the novel, Lydia Gwilt reads aloud to Midwinter a section from her diary, in which she reports her earlier reading of the text of "Armadale's Dream":

> "The darkness opened for the third time, and showed me the Shadow of the Man, and the Shadow of the Woman together. The Man-Shadow was the nearest; the Woman-Shadow stood back. From where she stood, I heard a sound like the pouring out of a liquid softly. I saw her touch the Shadow of the Man with one hand, and give him a glass with the other. He took the glass, and handed it to me."

The text then shifts frameworks as she continues, referring to the effect of the reading:

> "For the moment, I was as completely staggered by this extraordinary coincidence as Midwinter himself.
> "He put one hand on the open Narrative, and laid the other heavily on my arm." (563)

One hand on "narrative" and the other on a body, Midwinter's outstretched hands extend his own body in opposite directions, situating it in one of several "mid" spaces the novel constructs: between the text that opens up a space for character and the character who arrives to occupy it; between the dream and the ostensible reality to which it is said to refer; between the position and the person; between the text that "contains" a version of the real and the solidity of a body—even a dead one—whose existence would affirm that reality more securely. As his name suggests, Midwinter himself is a mediator: not only does he mediate Armadale's relation to Lydia and provide, most importantly at the novel's end, a bodily barrier between them, but he also mediates the idea of character itself, suggesting a midpoint between positionality and unique identity, sensationalism and realism. Like Lydia, he takes on different names and occupies numerous roles; unlike her, he seems to alter with each position, his "frenzy" among other signs of psychological depth suggesting both an interiority and an instability that set him apart from other characters.

As a bodily mediator, however, Midwinter in this moment of reaching between narrative and person epitomizes the function of other bodies in *Armadale*, for what I referred to earlier as the novel's mediation of its originary moments in fact takes shape as a layering of bodies: bodies through which texts must pass in order to be heard or read, to make their way to the narrative's surface in the form of written documents or spoken text (we might imagine Collins himself, reaching for the newspaper in which the story of the ship *The Armadale* is reported with one hand, and for his novel with the other). Why, one might reasonably ask, do we not read *Armadale* as a dream? For if the novel's reliance on the idea of suffocation, especially the locked-cabin scenario, seems dreamlike (and is, according to Freud, a common dream experience), it resembles the conventional idea of a dream in other ways as well: in, for instance, its very lack of coherence, the absence of what Bourne Taylor calls "stability" (writes Freud, "Dreams are disconnected, they accept the most violent contradictions without the least objection, they admit impossibilities. . . . Anyone who when he was awake behaved in the sort of way that is shown in situations in dreams would be considered insane" [87]). Midwinter's frenzied outburst or wandering about, having lost his way, might also be considered examples of "dreamlike" activity, as might the novel's proliferation of Armadales and layering of plots (see Freud 189). But we don't read *Armadale* as a dream, I would suggest, because we never see the body: we are never shown anyone dreaming it. What's missing, that is, is the framework: the idea of a dreamer, or simply the image of a sleeping body—a consciousness in which a dream may be imagined to be contained and through which it must pass before it surfaces in the form of narrative. Without such a frame, a dream must be—however sensational its content (as Collins's appendix suggests)—interchangeable with the real.

Many of the novel's key incidents and narratives are textually mediated, pointing toward Collins's—and sensation fiction's—characteristic awareness of the distance between what characters understand as the "real" and the ideological structures they inhabit. But more of its mediations are represented simply as relays or transmissions from one character to another. Rather than suggesting some alteration or possible alteration to the text, as stories of mediation might, that is, *Armadale* simply records a change in medium, a transfer of narrative, as in Armadale's account of Midwinter's transcription of his dream ("exactly what I dreamed"); events reported via Mrs. Oldershaw's letters and Lydia's diary; the account of the dying Armadale's letter to his son (in which nothing is made of any possible intervention by Mr. Neal, who fills in the blanks) and the written record of Armadale's dream. Mediation in these instances seems to have no point or purpose other than to gesture towards mediation: toward, that is, the narrative's journey through numerous hands and numerous bodies before it rises to the surface as "report"—as in the newspaper report of the ship's arrival, or the framing of numerous events as Lydia Gwilt's extensive diary entries.

In the theories of dream interpretation the novel invokes, including Hawbury's (and, in my analysis, Freud's), however, the passage of material through the body does have a transformative effect: the impression of mundane "irritants" or stimuli that penetrate the dreamer's consciousness tend to result not in dreams but in nightmares. Indeed, in another instance of mediation, these nightmare scenarios are the kinds of dreams Freud frequently selects from his sources as evidence for his own theories.

The rolling of thunder takes us into the thick of battle, the crow of a cock may be transformed into human shrieks of terror, and the creaking of a door may conjure up dreams of burglars breaking into the house. When one of our blankets slips off at night we may dream that we are walking about naked or falling into the water... Should our head accidentally get under the pillow we may then imagine a big rock hanging over us and about to crush us under its weight. (18)

Meier (1758, 33) once dreamt that he was overpowered by some men who stretched him out on his back on the ground and drove a stake into the earth between his big toe and the next one. While he was imagining this in the dream he woke up and found that a straw was sticking between his toes. On another occasion, according to Hennings (1784, 258), when Meier had fastened his shirt rather tight around his neck, he dreamt that he was being hanged. Hoffbauer (1796, 146) dreamt when he was a young man of falling down from a high wall, and when he woke up found that his bedstead had collapsed and that he had really fallen on to the floor. . . . Another man, who was sleeping with a hot poultice on his head, dreamt that he was being scalped by a band of Red Indians, while a third, who was wearing a damp nightshirt, imagined that he was being dragged through a stream. (58)

Freud cites a "celebrated" dream of Maury, one of his most prolific sources and dream experimenters:

He was sick, and remained in bed; his mother sat beside him. He then dreamed of the reign of terror at the time of the Revolution. He took part in terrible scenes of murder, and finally he himself was summoned before the Tribunal. . . . he was sentenced to death. Accompanied by an enormous crowd, he was led to the place of execution. He mounted the scaffold, the executioner tied him to the board, it tipped, and the knife of the guillotine fell. He felt his head severed from the trunk, and awakened in terrible anxiety, only to find that the top piece of the bed had fallen down, and had actually struck his cervical vertebra in the same manner as the knife of a guillotine. (21)

In most of these dreams (Maury's is an exception) small irritations or domestic annoyances—interruptions in a home imagined as functioning with an ideal smoothness (the same image of tranquility the novel's sanitorium projects as a cure for the madness caused by domestic disturbances)—have become terrors. Dreams are said to transform what might be regarded as minor and unavoidable domestic irritations into terrifying hallucinations: often, as in Maury's case, into an experience (as can be had only in dream or hallucination) of the subject's own death. Even the fly, that universal symbol of the irritatingly inconsequential, constitutes a serious disturbance, while a common matter such as a head shifting beneath the pillow rather than remaining atop it is fraught with danger, both imagined and—as in the case of Maury's broken bed—potentially real. (Not for nothing, then, does Midwinter reassure himself, as he waits for the outcome of the novel's final drama— Lydia's attempt to murder Armadale—"I can trust myself to stay awake" [659]). Given this theory, as I mentioned earlier, the drowning with which *Armadale* begins as well as the suffocation scenes with which it ends—including not only the attempted murder by poisoned air but the sanitorium director Dr. LeDoux's solution to domestic irritation, "suffocating" his patients in carefully controlled spaces—may all be imagined as dreams some external irritant could have produced.

The external irritant, in this interpretation, both explains the dream's terror and produces it. It serves as the dream's anchor in the real, reassuring the dreamer that "the mind has remained in constant communication with the material world even during sleep" (17). For Dr. LeDoux, however, such irritations are the source of his patients' madness. The sanitorium thus has as its chief curative method the maintaining of an atmosphere free from such domestic irritants, removing not those nightmare-like anxieties in which sensation fiction famously trades, such as murder and bigamy, but rather those annoyances of the specific variety that, LeDoux asserts, can drive a person mad: the annoyances of ordinary domestic life. "Find a door banging in *this* house, if you can! Catch a servant in *this* house, rattling the tea-things when he takes away the tray!" Indeed, pulling a handle from without to close a window and seal off the room while the patient is snug in bed (626), the doctor not only eliminates the banal annoyances that constitute daily life, but in doing so reproduces the nightmare of the locked cabin. The notion that dreams are grounded in the real is thus a reassuring sign of continued connection to the real and an exposure of the banal real as a death-trap, in which sleep becomes a rehearsal or staging ground for death. (It is hardly surprising, especially after going over only a few of this novel's complicated plot points, that a contemporary critic described the entire thing as a bad dream: *Armadale*, proposed a reviewer for the *Saturday Review*, has the effect of a "literary nightmare," making readers "feel uncomfortable without letting them know why" (Bourne Taylor 154).

Moreover, despite Freud's point that the dream is not just an indiscriminate response to stimuli (that the individual's consciousness responds to some stimuli, such as the calling of one's name, and not to others; that the dream is shaped by internal processes as well as external ones), the dreams he describes possess a generic quality; indeed, Freud may be credited (though *The Interpretation* cites numerous co-workers in the field) with having produced a new genre. Since any such coding or hypothesis of genre filters out some details in favor of others, the dream-as-genre is a way of stabilizing—rendering part of the real—the dream's unsettling instabilities: screening out of interpretation, and indeed possibly of perception and/or memory, any details that do not fit its rubric.[21] In other words, the dream, like sensation fiction, is at its foundation a realist text. It makes sense, then, that reported dreams play such a key role in Freud's *Interpretation*, for the text can only work as a set of rules or code-book if the dreams reported and the signs to be interpreted within them are recognizable and translatable: like Oedipus and his commonplace complex, they must in theory belong to everyone.

Not only does dream transformation have a specific kind of content, then—the transformation of the trivial into the terrible—but that content must also be generic: something anyone may experience. And not only does this analysis make the dream into a genre, but it also makes dreams in some sense *about* genre, since their function is to transform the ordinary—a banal if irritating (or perhaps irritating because banal) collection of realist details—into a terrifying but much more interesting drama: something like the drama that characterizes sensation fiction. The unique individual becomes irrelevant, as does the nature of the detail; both are subordinated to the genre, in which what is revealed—as the nature of the dream, but also as the dreamer's unwitting artistry, power, and depth—is the transformation of realist detail into sensational narrative. Though dreams provided psychoanalysis with the material to produce the deeply interiorized characters of realist fiction, the analysis of dreams codifies interiority, producing dreams that adhere to already established rules.

In this context, the layering of bodies that functions in this text as an image of mediation is relevant to the idea of the dream as well as to that of sensation fiction, and ultimately to the idea of genre as well, for what individual persons become, in the context of genre theory as well as ideology—given that we understand genres as ideological formations—are genre machines or mediators: sites for transforming one genre (or reality) into another. And if, as I have suggested, Collins's novel dreams of the real, it may also be the case that, like the often terrifying expressions of ordinary consciousness such dreams (as theory has it) turn out to be, sensation fiction is a realist dream, or a realist's: the expression of any ordinary person's unaccountable and sometimes terrifying unconscious, in terms that the conscious mind—the person in his or her waking state—can nevertheless understand. The sensational dream, like sensation fiction, in this reading, is an intensification and transformation of the real but not really a betrayal of it: it is a realist (and realist's) fantasy, enlivening ordinary existence even as it makes the dreamer a function of genres and their attendant ideologies.

That is: the mundane or everyday realist detail may provide a reassuring, stabilizing context for what are, certainly in Freud's accounts, a collection of terrifying scenarios; it may also serve, as in the case of the ship called *The Armadale,* as well as Žižek's comment about the relation between illusion and the real, as an unsettling mirror of it, suggesting that the real can dream of sensation fiction just as sensation fiction dreams of the real. The permeability of the self—and what we might at this point call the generic undecidability of the self—resolved by psychoanalysis into the categories of waking and sleep or reality and dream, and by literary history into classifications such as realism and sensation fiction, is all too visible in *Armadale*'s watery and unsettled landscape, as in its characters' preternatural awareness and embodiment of both sensational and realist conventions.

As my initial discussion of Collins's gestures toward the real suggested, another undecidable category with reference to the relation between dreams and the external world is time. Rational dream theory makes it possible, as I suggested above and as common experience has it, that the dreamer's experience of time distorts, by seeming to lengthen, the dream's duration. If a dream is provoked, for example, by a passing siren or the sound of an alarm clock, a narrative that ends with some similar noise—waking the dreamer—must have been extremely compressed or accelerated, however long it seemed to take; it must also have preceded the event that seems to provoke it. But there is another issue here as well, involving the relation of the dream's end to the experience that precedes it, and bearing both on the questions *Armadale* raises about free will and about the ending-after-the-ending that Collins offers in the form of the novel's appendix. For the rational theory of dreams—the idea that dreams arise from external stimulation—raises the issue not so much of the way the past or the dream forecloses or determines the future as it does the possibility that the present or future might determine, and indeed produce, what we understand the past to be: if rationality arrives in the form of an alarm clock or the ship called *The Armadale*, that arrival tells us not (or not only) where our dream narrative began but also where it must end. Mimicking, in the form of an afterword, the afterwardsness that structures dreams (the afterword announcing the existence of the real ship, that is, as the literary form of afterwardsness), Collins "frames" his own novel—and seeks to affirm its value—by reaching for a reality outside it. But the coincidence of the ships' names—life imitating art, as the saying goes—also affirms the inability of the real to remain within its generic boundaries.

That the present might predict or shape the past sheds further light on *Armadale*'s layers of mediation as well as its mythic echoes, given the characteristic relation between psychoanalysis and myth, in which the individual "discovers" or recognizes in his present life the recapitulation of his own history, and of a mythic history whose origins seem to recede, potentially forever, backwards in time. The question *Armadale* raises about Armadale's dream—does it predict the future, or can I shape it myself?—is the same question, Freud claimed, we all ask when we interrogate our own origins, and discover in the endless possibilities for narrative construction that project affords, as well as in its recapitulation of an already-known and often quite sensational story, the same problem that confronts Collins's Allan Armadales, and indeed all Armadales everywhere.

Armadale's dreams—not just that of the novel's central character, but its use of dreams and dream theory in general—attend to realist details in a manner that transforms their size and significance. Making the buzzing flies or rattling tea-trays of domestic life into matters of life and death, the dream performs the same generic task as sensation fiction, taking realism to extremes and in the process emphasizing the life-and-death significance of its trivial sources: the opening or closing of windows; the shifting of pillows and blankets; the clatter of tea trays: "events in themselves harmless, which his [Midwinter's] superstition had distorted from their proper shape" (280). The logic of enlarging domestic annoyances or "irritants" extends to the status of identity: when the small detail becomes extraordinary the ordinary self does as well, becoming, in effect, more of a player in a life-and-death drama than a nuanced and unique individual. But the novel also reverses this enlargement or sensationalization, making the ostensibly small and "real" into an object of desire. Despite her contempt for the ordinary, for instance, Lydia Gwilt dreams of being Miss Milroy, seeking to reproduce in her own story a romance to match that of Allan and his fiancé while using the category of "irritant" to distinguish herself from those ostensibly insipid others whose ideology she is nevertheless looking to imitate. The "irritant"—as represented here not only by Milroy and Armadale but also by the breaking down of ordinary domesticity—defines a realm of insignificance inseparable from ideology: like the things of thing theory, it becomes an annoyance only when it breaks down, suggesting the seriousness of any disruption of the built system and ideological scenarios it helps to maintain.

As a vehicle for transforming irritating banalities into sensational drama, the dreamer in *Armadale* becomes a figure for narrative transformation, with dreams themselves said to be a reaction—albeit unconscious—to the proprieties of realist ideology and their accompanying discontents. The claim that dreams are provoked by external incidents reproduces Collins's implicit argument, in *Armadale*'s appendix, for the realism of his own text; his account of the existence of an actual ship named *The Armadale* mirrors dream theory's attempts to settle the instabilities and uncertainties of dreams by anchoring them in the real. And yet that anchor repeatedly suggests its own failure, not only because of the generic instability the ship's story reinforces (it is no more "real" than it is "sensational") but also in the necessity of finding a rationale—a source in the external real—for the heightened awareness of a continuously sleeping subject, as well as in the need to explain the seeming illogic according to which, as dream theory has it, a later event can provoke an earlier one. If the first necessity hardly conceals its ideological intentions—a nightmare is said to be provoked by bad management in the form of a domestic disturbance—the reliability of the latter can be guaranteed only by ongoing attempts to stabilize the instabilities of dreams.

Character here is not the center from which everything derives, as realist ideology would suggest, but rather a framework or medium: for genre, for ideology, for the transformation of one genre or ideology into another. The dreamer's body in *Armadale*, then, along with the numerous characters in the novel who function as mediators of narrative and story, resembles the window frames and doorways in *Adam Bede* and *The Return of the Native*, or the mirror in *The Woodlanders*: all are frameworks that allow for shifts in meaning as the novel oscillates between registers—enabling readers to see them and see through them, as they provide access to the novels' generic and ideological claims. Thus the woman in the window or doorway is both significantly a character—Adam's mother Lisbeth, Dinah Morris, and now, Lydia Gwilt—and a template, exchangeable for and interchangeable with other women. In these moments and figures, realism's emphasis on character reproduces sensation fiction's emphasis on position in a manner that the realist novel's individualistic ethos does not acknowledge or endorse.

In these readings, the character's body becomes realism's figurative home: the structure that supports its illusions. As in Bourdieu's account of the way bodily memories, like the Kabyle house, embody cultural customs and practices imperceptibly so that their cultural status and essential arbitrariness can be forgotten, so too do these texts animate their characters, telling them to walk this way; to go downstairs; to press their noses against window panes, or simply to peer in. These characters are shaped and inhabited by genre and its attendant ideologies rather than the other way around, dreaming of the real and encouraging us to do the same.

Chapter 6

Conclusion
Critical Desire and the Victorian Real

I have been arguing that the signal conventions of the Victorian realist novel, as well as conventions unique to particular texts (whether those texts are typically called realist or not) define a desire for the real and mark the category of the real as a Victorian object of desire. If dreams and fantasies are often described as, well, fantastic—easily distinguishable from the rule-bound, organized, and regulated realm that tends to be associated with the real—these novelists and characters dream, by contrast, of the ordinary: of demands, distinctions, classifications, prohibitions. What novels situate as dream or fantasy overlaps with, and is often indistinguishable from, conventional realist forms; it may also be imagined as a transformation of them, in structures such as sensation fiction and dreams, whose origins are said to be grounded in the real and therefore recoverable by retracing, and thereby reinscribing as solid and unchanging, the details of ordinary everyday life.

My argument has not been about the relation between literary classifications such as the Gothic, the fantastic, fairy-tale or romance, on the one hand, and realism on the other, except to suggest that such codified differences—as in the case of the distinction between realism and sensation fiction—resemble distinctions between levels or kinds of consciousness in the process of being firmed up at the same historical moment. The distinction between realism and sensation fiction, as I have suggested, plays out and indeed reinforces, in the realm of literary criticism, Freud's distinction between those kinds of representations staged by the conscious mind and those staged by the unconscious. Indeed, dream interpretation's translation of symbolic or coded discourse into coherent psychological narrative is the project of much sensation fiction, which solves its baffling mysteries by revealing buried genealogies and decoding signs. To say this is not to claim that one form of cultural discourse discovered what another then reified, but rather to point out that asserted differences between codes and elements aligned with consciousness, on the one hand, and with unconsciousness on the other—based on the kinds of narratives each mode is said to produce, and the techniques marshaled to "translate" one mode into the other (and indeed the perceived necessity of such translation)—may also be described as differences in genre, and thus perceived less as unchangeable realities than as effects of cultural classification. Conceiving of genres as, in effect, projections of the self, this shift in interpretation and terminology emphasizes the nature of the asserted differences or oppositions between genres not as a choice between the real and the unreal, the actual and the fantastic, but rather as a choice of fantasies. In one, the human subject participates in a logical, linear narrative and is in control of the objects that surround him or her (viewed as components of a manageable, everyday domesticity), while in the other the individual falls prey to the power of such objects—no longer "ordinary"—and loses control as well of his or her internal impulses and surrounding environment. This choice is itself an ideological one in which the mind, like the novel, is said to be divided into opposing camps: the one said to exemplify a realist impulse while the other is called primitive, uncontrolled, or simply whimsical. In this final chapter, I want to suggest that contemporary criticism, and in particular criticism of Victorian fiction, has yet to leave such ideologically-loaded distinctions behind. Surface reading, for instance, along with other forms of criticism that make claims for accuracy and objectivity, continue a Victorian tradition of founding ideological distinctions on putative differences between what is said to be real and what is held to be, by contrast, merely whimsical or fantastic. In doing so—in claiming to take us from critical fantasy or mere subjectivity to a stable reality—they recapitulate the pattern of novelistic realist conventions I have discussed throughout this book, asserting and not significantly updating what is perhaps the most general articulation of Victorian realist fantasy: the idea of seeing things "as they really are."

In their introduction to an influential issue of *Representations* called "The Way We Read Now" (2009), Sharon Marcus and Stephen Best claim that what they dub "symptomatic" or "suspicious" reading is Victorian at its roots.[1] They argue that a mode of reading in which the critic looks "beneath" a text's surface for hidden meanings may be traced to Marxist notions of mystification and Freudian ideas of the unconscious, both nineteenth-century master narratives of symptom and suspicion later shifted to the political realm by a series of literary theorists, most prominently, in their account, Fredric Jameson. But the rhetoric of their manifesto echoes another, unacknowledged Victorian master narrative: the ideal of objectivity, as articulated in particular by Matthew Arnold. The idea that critics should seek to "describe texts accurately," to "see more clearly," and to provide "a more complete view of reality" recalls Arnold's definition of culture, which he saw as "disinterestedly trying, in its aim at perfection, to see things as they really are" (23). Arnold defined culture as the opposite of anarchy, and for him the alternative to seeing things as they really are, or what he called Hellenism (defined as sweetness and light, beauty, intelligence, and the "spontaneity of consciousness" [110]—the program of personal cultivation and development that ultimately allows us to be our best selves), was what he dubbed Hebraism, characterized by anarchy, violence, and destruction. Marcus and Best do not go this far in their echo of Arnold. But the parallels between their language and his recalls the way in which claims to see things "best" or "as they really are" require the evocation of some alternative, necessarily occluded form of vision—in this case, in a manner relevant both to Arnold's argument and to the idea of surface reading, one said to be clouded by emotionality (as the use of the terms "suspicion" and "symptom" suggest) and marked by an absence of self-restraint. If the desire to contest the taken-for-granted assertion of power enabled by such Arnoldian assertions about truth—the idea that we could have it, if only we saw things in the right way—once made suspicious readers like Marx and Freud so necessary and so welcome, surface reading reverses this idea, turning one stream of Victorian thought against another, without, however, noting the historical context of the second, so that this claim seems to stand on its own as the assertion of a universal and self-evident truth. That is, the rhetoric of surface reading's manifesto reproduces realism's claim to transparency, defining itself as free of conventions, values, and agendas other than the desire for a more accurate and (hence) better kind of reading.

This rhetoric about the clear-sightedness associated with "surface" details, reminiscent of realism's own use of the rhetoric of visuality, also echoes what Lorraine Daston and Peter Galison have described as the Victorian moralization of objectivity—or more precisely what they call "mechanical" objectivity, in which a technology such as photography is valued because it seems to provide a way to avoid the interference of an unruly self in the act of analysis, offering "the promise of images uncontaminated by interpretation."[2] As Daston and Galison argue, Victorian objectivity was a claim of victory in the struggle against inner enemies such as imagination and individual judgment. "Although mechanical objectivity was nominally in the service of truth to nature," they write, "its primary allegiance was to a morality of self-restraint" (117). This idealization and moralization of objectivity as self-restraint carries over to Marcus and Best, whose manifesto is an assault on previous modes of reading, and who judge critics who do not take a text at "face value" to be suspicious, aggressive, and in "attack" mode.[3] Indeed, the terms "suspicious" and "symptomatic" fill the role of Hebraism here, locating specific modes of reading and those who employ them on the wrong side of a moral divide.

Marcus and Best suggest that one way to perform surface reading is to locate gaps in textual surfaces, filling in areas whose contents remain invisible to the naked eye. But the logic they use to introduce this idea is indistinguishable from a description of reading for depth: "the most significant truths," they suggest, "are not immediately apprehensible and may be veiled or invisible" (4). Or this: "what lies in plain sight is worthy of attention but often eludes observation" (18). Or: "to see more clearly does not require that we plumb hidden depths" (18). The rhetoric of locating invisible truths on the surface sounds no different from the rhetoric of suspicious or deep reading, which needs to go "beneath" in order to find out secrets; the difference is merely rhetorical, and sometimes not even that. What remains unchanged is the claim to see more clearly, to see things "as they really are." And in fact the rhetoric of depth versus surface is a diversion from the visual metaphor that in fact structures this discussion: the idea that it is possible to see clearly and hence truly, to rid vision of frameworks and contexts.

By situating the idea of objectivity within the Victorian discourse of self-restraint, Daston and Galison demonstrate just how ideologically saturated the idea of clear vision, of seeing things accurately, always is. This other Victorianism—the one Marcus and Best do not discuss— was and remains ideological; the purpose of the Holmesian claim that the evidence speaks for itself, if we only possess the eye trained to see it, is always the convicting of the guilty party. For it is not the idea of depth that involves asserting mastery over the text, nor does the idea of surface reading offer an escape from that dynamic. It is, rather, the rhetoric of clear vision—the idea of seeing things as they really are, of laying claim to the real—that is always and inescapably an assertion of power, and in this sense there is no difference between Arnold's rhetoric and Marcus and Best's. Reading for what is called "surface" is no less a gesture of mastery than the idea of reading for depth; claims for surface reading, like claims for new modes of interpretation, justify a change in technique by claiming that it provides a greater purchase on the real than previous critical modes. Indeed, the impulse behind what surface readers are reacting to—symptomatic or "suspicious" reading—was realist as well, in its insistence that fictional narrative obscured stories about actual material and social conditions. For Marxist and Freudian readers, realist narrative obscures uncomfortable contradictions that their critical methods expose.

Marcus and Best's manifesto is oddly prohibitive: its purchase on criticism is made via a warning against certain kinds of interpretation— really, against interpretation itself—as condensed in their slogan, "just read" (12). Like the Nike advertisement it echoes ("just do it"), the admonishment equates minimalism and simplicity with truth: if you are doing more than "reading," which the phrase implicitly contrasts with interpreting ("innocent" reading is defined by the minimalist suggestion of "just," as if to suggest a kind of reading that unthinkingly digests the written word), you are by definition overreading, performing some activity not suitably captured by the ostensibly self-evident sufficiency of the term. Reading is imagined as ideally and potentially theory-free, untainted by critical frameworks. Surface reading, like the denotative reading theorized by Cannon Schmitt and Elaine Freedgood in a subsequent move to bring criticism closer to the "real" of the text, promotes an ideal in which it is thought possible (and this is the critical dream these efforts represent) to bring words into a closer proximity with the things they name (hence the valorizing of the term "denotation").[4] And yet all reading—I want to say "of course" here, though clearly not everyone agrees—relies on interpretive activity of the kind "just reading" would seem to want to exclude. In reaching for the real, then, surface reading finds itself relying on the kinds of prohibitive structures I have discussed in other chapters in relation to representations of the real, and condemning what it construes as the alternative: a kind of reading described as fantasmatic for its inability to see things "as they really are."[5] And yet the desire for a reading method free of frameworks, contexts, and theory is similarly inflected with fantasy, its purpose seeming to have less to do with a desire for truth than with a blurring, shared by realism as well, between description and prescription. Realism's desirability—and that of the idea of the real itself—comes in part from its perceived ability to tell us what to do: in this case, how to read. For it only makes sense: to do anything other than access the real flies in the face of the empiricism on which, Watt reminds us, the novel itself based its claims to truth, and the morality that aligns being right with seeing right.

A contest between discourses of fantasy and those of the ostensibly real as inflected by spatial metaphors of surface and depth plays out in a Victorian text that takes on the difficult-to-escape whimsy of the metaphorically "deep": Darwin's *Expression of the Emotions in Man and Animals* (1872). Darwin, a surface reader *avant la lettre*, argued that signs normally understood as expressions of emotion were in fact vestiges or traces of actions useful to our animal ancestors but no longer serving any purpose. He argued, that is, against any kind of depth other than the historical and biological: in expressions of emotion, he claimed, we see only an image of our biological/historical past. What he calls "grief muscles," for example, as manifested in the drawing down of the eyebrows, exist to protect the eyes from pain; any tears that emerge are there to wash out some foreign substance. Darwin famously thus looked to expression not for meaning but for its absence: like a surface reader, he argued that the signs we see have no "deep" meaning but are rather the traces of some instinctive physical response. His purpose, we might say, was to take the depth out of something commonly understood only as an expression of depth: human emotion. And part of his method of doing so, as in the case of the argument for surface reading, involved making a case for the superiority of one form of interpretation over another: in this instance, again as in surface reading, a presumably dispassionate, scientific way of reading is opposed to one that, especially because it involved the interpretation of emotion, would not be capable of seeing clearly.

Darwin believed that some muscles were under "greater control of the will"[6] than others, and hence could be used to dissimulate. And indeed much of his discussion notes instances in which will or "habit" somehow alter or interfere with an instinctive response that would otherwise emerge unmediated (190). By way of illustration, he ends his chapter on expressions of grief and anxiety with the following "trifling observation," a description of a woman seated opposite him on a train.

Whilst I was looking at her, I saw that her *depressoris anguli oris* became very slightly, yet decidedly, contracted; but as her countenance remained as placid as ever, I reflected how meaningless was this contraction, and how easily one might be deceived. The thought had hardly occurred to me when I saw that her eyes suddenly became suffused with tears almost to overflowing, and her whole countenance fell. There could now be no doubt that some painful recollection, perhaps that of a long-lost child, was passing through her mind. As soon as her sensorium was thus affected, certain nerve-cells from long habit instantly transmitted an order to all the respiratory muscles, and to those round the mouth, to prepare for a fit of crying. But the order was countermanded by the will, or rather by a later acquired habit, and all the muscles were obedient, excepting in a slight degree the *depressoris anguli oris*. The mouth was not even opened; the respiration was not hurried; and no muscle was affected except those which draw down the corners of the mouth. (193)

The action he describes, Darwin goes on to say, would appear differently were the woman's powers of interference less developed; the "rudimentary vestiges of the screaming-fits" (194) on display in infancy would be that much more pronounced. What he describes as "meaninglessness" is in fact a record of conflict: an image of the command center at work on its unruly subject, putting down a minor rebellion on the part of the *depressoris anguli oris* ("all the muscles," he notes admiringly, "were obedient"). Darwin sees in this woman's expression what is for him a timeless or universal battle between self-control and unruliness: the action of the facial muscles, one set emerging to check the other, tell the story of a struggle between the civilized self and the infant or primitive one.

The passage recalls the description of Lady Mason's face I discussed in my chapter on *Orley Farm*.

> Yes; she would still bear up. . . . She would dress herself with care, and go down into the court with a smooth brow. Men, as they looked at her, should not at once say, "Behold the face of a guilty woman!". . . But the absolute bodily labour which she was forced to endure was so hard upon her! She would dress herself, and smooth her brow for the trial; but that dressing herself, and that maintenance of a smooth brow would impose upon her an amount of toil which would almost overtask her physical strength. . . . She longed for rest, to be able to lay aside the terrible fatigue of being ever on the watch. (2:232)

Lady Mason, as we know, has forged the signature to a will so that her son Lucius will inherit property that should actually go to her former husband. The novel does not hinge on the question of her innocence or guilt—readers know the answer to that—but rather on the way other characters respond to her: whether they consider her innocent or guilty or something else altogether; how, thinking one way or another, they think of her. Like so many of Trollope's characters, she is right in one context and wrong in another; between those poles of innocence and guilt lie numerous moral, ethical, and psychological shadings. But those who surround her for the most part remain unaware of such subtleties; for them, she is an object of suspicion. What for Darwin's train companion is an almost unconscious reflex, the self-control anyone might exercise in a public place, has for Lady Mason been a twenty-years-long ordeal. Preparing to meet the suspicious crowd requires her constant attention: the perpetual effort of superimposing the innocent face over the guilty one. And what interests the novelist, like the scientist, are the traces of that labor: ever vigilant, Lady Mason is also unbearably fatigued, and despite her vigilance knows she can only delay the exposure that is the inevitable result of being surrounded by suspicious face-readers: "Men, as they looked at her, should not *at once* say, behold the face of a guilty woman." What they should see, and indeed admire, Trollope suggests, is the effort invested in maintaining the surface: the nobility expressed not in the action, but in the exertion of bearing up: the strength it took and continues to take to be Lady Mason.

The subject who layers one expression over another—innocence over guilt, seriousness over mirth, contentment over pain—has perhaps no depth but only surface, only behavior. The structure of a face thus described recalls that of sedimentary rock as described by Charles Lyell: it's all surfaces, all the way down. And yet Darwin, clearly doing more than "just" reading, finds the story he is looking for, though the actual nature of that story, within a range of possible, acceptable, and indeed ideologically appropriate stories ("perhaps" the woman is grieving a long-lost child) matters less than the claim that there is one. The structure of the activity itself—looking, interpreting, naming—is a claim to mastery and, as such, an assertion that some elements of interpretation are more pertinent than others: identifying the *depressos anguli oris*, crucial; identifying the cause of what might also be called an expression of grief, not so crucial, and yet also not wholly irrelevant.[7]

In this narrative, and even more in the impulse to tell it, it is as if the scientist's unruly self—the one that wants to tell a story, perhaps because he senses the presence of something other than the vestige of an animal past—briefly slips out: hence, one might argue, the similarity between the scientist's analysis and the novelist's. The story Darwin reads in this woman's face, embroidering upon what it perhaps seems too heartless to describe as a mere action of the facial muscles, is—despite his claim for its universality—a brief moment of unscientific identification in which the scientist glimpses an unruly face that in its struggle (and in the struggle it represents between different discourses) reflects the scientist's battle with his own unruly impulses. Seeing in the face that he reads a struggle between impulse and self-control, a battle in which the unruly self meets a will that countermands it, what Darwin sees, I want to suggest, is the struggle over scientific objectivity writ large; the face becomes the site on which the contest between impulse and self-restraint plays itself out. As the markers of the "real" for Darwin—the movements of the woman's musculature—segue seamlessly into a fantasy about her interior life, the woman emerges as a realist fantasy: a figure reflecting Darwin's wishes and desires for his own method and signaling at the same time that method's inability to prohibit the scientist's own thoughts, indeed, his own struggles, from shaping his observations. That Trollope writes that same struggle into Lady Mason's face suggests not that the novelist is engaged in any kind of "objective" pursuit, but rather that both the scientist and the novelist are engaged in what is typically called a novelistic one, and that science too is a way of reading, for surface or for depth, that, like any projection of desire, sees a reflection of its own face in the faces that it sees.

The struggle between impulse and the will, or between a desire to control and the inability to do so, appears in *Armadale* as Midwinter's defining characteristic; it is what divides this "wild" character from his near-twin, the sedate and civilized Alan Armadale, and also what distinguishes the horrific backstory—the story in which one man locks another in a sinking ship's cabin—from the polite domestic drama of his descendant's bourgeois courtship and marriage. It provides, as I have pointed out, the framework of Daston and Galison's account of Victorian objectivity, which accused unruly emotions of interfering with the ability to see things clearly and see them whole. This is the ideology that surfaces in surface reading, as well as in other accounts that, taking up the quest for a new, less whimsical form of reading while seeking to avoid surface reading's pitfalls, reproduce a binary distinction between readings said to be "accurate" and other presumably less-accurate modes of interpretation. My purpose throughout this book has been to attempt to show, by reading the realist novel's desire for the real—and inevitable participation in a dream of the real—that all such distinctions and definitions are similarly fantasmatic products of a wish to separate that which can be counted on, grounded in the real and substantial, from the (by contrast) illusory and insubstantial. And the desire to discover what can be counted on, in both genres—the novelistic and the critical—manifests itself as instruction, and more than that, prescription. The desire for the real is also a desire to be told what to do, and the motivating idea offered for critical formulations of the real, from Matthew Arnold to surface reading, is that we cannot but choose to follow instructions that show us the way to the real; that, indeed, there is no other morally responsible choice. The opposition between accuracy and whimsy can have no other point or purpose, and its moralism is inherently—historically—Victorian. And what persists within this narrative—what occupies the position of the "real"—is not impulse, on the one hand, or the desire for control on the other, but the premise that there is an ongoing struggle between the two.

In the essay "Mr. Bennett and Mrs. Brown" (1923), Virginia Woolf describes witnessing a conversation on a train between an elderly woman, whom she calls Mrs. Brown, and an elderly man, whom she calls Mr. Smith; Smith appears "to have some power over her [Mrs. Brown] that he was exerting disagreeably." [8] As they speak, Woolf writes, "a very odd thing happened. Mrs. Brown took out her little white handkerchief and began to dab her eyes. She was crying." After Smith disembarks, Woolf imagines the events that might have led up to their dispute, responding to the "impression she [Mrs. Brown] made": "She sat in her corner opposite, very clean, very small, rather queer, and suffering intensely. The impression she made was overwhelming" (30). "The story ends without any point to it," she writes. But it does in fact have a point, and a very large one: "all novels," she claims, "begin with an old lady in the corner opposite" She elaborates by making Mrs. Brown an exemplar of "character," which, she claims, the novel form "has evolved" to express (30–31). But in light of the passages by Darwin and Trollope discussed above, one might hazard that there is something more specific about a woman on a train as an initiatory figure for the novel—and perhaps also for the dispute Woolf stages here between the novelist Arnold Bennet (let's call him Smith), whom she offers as an example of a writer interested only in surface, and herself, for whom the novel must be a study of depth. As a figure who is assumed to feel deeply, that is, the woman on the train is subject to the constraints that accompany a Victorian woman in public and, as the example of Lady Mason suggests, in private as well. This figure again epitomizes the quintessential Victorian struggle between impulse and restraint, and as such becomes, like the woman in Darwin's text, an opportunity for novelistic activity on the part of the observer: she is already a character, already a story. In fact, describing Mrs. Brown as "one of those clean, threadbare old ladies whose extreme tidiness . . . suggests more extreme poverty than rags and dirt," Woolf makes use of the same realist convention Eliot deploys for Mr. Irwine ("one of those men who . . ."); she relies, like a good realist novelist, on the metonymic fantasy that ties persons to their realist effects. Like Trollope's Lady Mason and Darwin's woman on the train, Mrs. Brown is someone we already know when we see her, condensing in her own figure—as Woolf both perceives and imagines her—the positionality of sensation fiction's characters and the unique status of realism's. It is possible, that is, to be both; it is, in fact, perhaps impossible for a novelistic character not to be both a bearer of ideology's effects as well as the novelist's unique production.[9] In the hands of a novelist, Mrs. Brown becomes another example (following those by Eliot, Hardy, Collins and Darwin) of a woman in a frame: an image of the ideological structuring of realist representation. Like the woman who captures Darwin's attention, however, she is interesting precisely because she both invites and resists such reduction. Though her ordinary, solid, and familiar surface invites the imagining of a story that might well be hers, she is and must remain a realist fantasy.

NOTES

Introduction

1. My use of the term "fantasy" generally follows Žižek's in his discussion of ideology and Lacan: ideology, Žižek argues, is "a fantasy-construction which serves as a support for our 'reality' itself: an 'illusion' which structures our effective, real social relations and thereby masks some insupportable, real, impossible kernel." Žižek, *Sublime*, 45. I am not concerned here with the nature of the kernel, but rather with the idea that this "fantasy construction" offers a coherent system of representations accepted as a common reality.

2. Barthes, "Reality Effect." Seminal work in this area includes Barthes, *S/Z*; MacCabe, *Tracking the Signifier*, 33–57; Belsey, *Critical Practice*; Jameson, *Political Unconscious*; and Miller, *The Novel and the Police*.

3. "There can be no realism unless the reader simultaneously sees the glass and pretends that he does not see it." Kendrick, *Novel-Machine*, 6–7; Žižek, *Sublime*, 45. It is true that Kendrick does not really say that the glass disappears, but says rather that the reader "pretends" not to see it; my sense, however, is that when readers assent to the reality or accuracy of realist conventions they agree to a consensus about the real. The level of pretending or making-believe involved may be complex and is certainly debatable.

4. One might cite in this context the reliance on empirical data and linear narrative that structures numerous disciplines, including medicine and the law, as well as the way in which, as critics are increasingly recognizing, convictions about the nature of interiority and character may not so much provide a basis for fictional representation as derive from it. On subjectivity as a literary effect, for instance, see Freedgood, "The Novelist and Her Poor";

on the mutually-constituted fictiveness of "world and book," see Christoff, "Alone with *Tess*." In a question about *Tess* that has implications on the way we conceive of our relation to fictional characters, Christoff asks, "To the people around us, isn't our interiority as fictional as a literary character's? And aren't we just as prone to thinking of our life stories in terms of literary convention?" (28).

5. Arnold, *Culture and Anarchy*, 23; Daston and Galison, *Objectivity*, 17; 122; Batchelor, review of Laurie Langbauer, *Novels of Everyday Life*.

6. Althusser, "Ideology and Ideological State Apparatuses." Other, related discussions of the imaginary which have informed my thinking include Dror Wahrman's work on the discourses that dismantle the "reality" of what is generally understood as the middle class, and Carolyn Steedman's account of the way social class permeates representations of the real. Steedman's narratives of class identity—as in her discussion of the family romance crucial to my reading of *Oliver Twist*—make it amply apparent how imbricated in one another are the modes we call "realism" and "fantasy," and to what extent the first term may be aligned, as Wahrman argues, less with any indisputable reality than with consensus: a general agreement to accept a set of terms, conditions, and/or institutions. Warman, *Imagining the Middle Class*; Steedman, "True Romance."

7. Eliot, *Adam Bede*, 185.

8. This describes what goes by the name of "classic realism," as discussed by Belsey and MacCabe. The dominant articulation of this definition is Ian Watt's, in *The Rise of the Novel*. But accounts of realism that define it as an attempt to represent some empirical reality or truth are numerous. They range, to cite only a few examples, from George Levine's assertion that the term realism "always implies an attempt to use language to get beyond language, to discover some nonverbal truth out there," or, more recently, "Nineteenth-century realism . . . leans toward the scrupulous construction of social and historical context as it impinges on the lives of characters"; *Realistic Imagination*, 6; "Literary Realism Reconsidered," in Beaumont, *Adventures in Realism*, 18, to Ruskinian realism as discussed by Caroline Levine in *Serious Pleasures of Suspense*. Weinstein's *Unknowing: The Work of Modernist Fiction*, 49–76, is a lucid and helpful guide to realist assumptions in the context of post-modern critiques.

9. A rhetoric of unmasking, led by Macherey's *Theory of Literary Production*, Jameson's *Political Unconscious*, and Miller's *The Novel and the Police* has dominated criticism of the Victorian realist novel over the past few decades; a reaction against it, as in what has been called "suspicious" or "symptomatic" reading, has produced a variety of counter-approaches; see Marcus and Best, "Surface Reading."

10. I am not referring to the inevitable "doubleness" involved in reading fiction: the suspension of disbelief that inevitably occurs when we read, as analyzed, for instance, by Newsom in *A Likely Story* and by Schor, *Curious Subjects*. While reading fiction obviously includes some general notion of fantasy—as in imagining oneself in a situation not one's own—my argument requires the elements of wish fulfillment and ideological substitution that the term "fiction" does not imply.

11. Grenier, *Sympathetic Realism in Nineteenth-Century British Fiction*, 57 and elsewhere.

12. On length and seriality in Trollope's fiction, see Langbauer, *Novels of Everyday Life*.

13. Watt, *Rise of the Novel*; Jakobson, "Metaphoric and Metonymic Poles"; Brooks, *Realist Vision*, 16; Barthes, "Reality Effect."

14. MacCabe has pointed out that the idea of the real is "tied to a particular type of literary production—the nineteenth-century realist novel. The dominance of this form is such that people still tend to confuse the general question of realism with the particular form of the nineteenth-century realist novel." *Tracking*, 35.

15. An exception would be an analysis such as Belsey's which describes what realism does rather than what it is.

16. Belsey, *Critical Practice*, 56–84; MacCabe, *Tracking the Signifier*, 33–57; Miller, *Novel and the Police*; Lynch, *Economy of Character*; Woloch, *One vs. the Many*; Matz, *Satirical Realism*; Ermarth, *Realism and Consensus*; Armstrong, *Fiction in the Age of Photography*; Freedgood, *Ideas in Things*; Hadley, *Living Liberalism*; Menke, *Telegraphic Realism*; Jameson, *Antinomies of Realism*.

17. My alignment of realism and fantasy might also suggest a comparison wih Srdan Smajic's article, "Supernatural Realism." My use of the term "fantasy" refers, however, not to the supernatural but rather to any individual's ordinary desires. Smajic, "Supernatural Realism."

18. Bourdieu, *Outline of a Theory of Practice*, 91.

19. Armstrong, *How Novels Think*, 17.

20. Hawthorne's remark appears in Trollope, *Autobiography* 144. "Just read" appears in Sharon Marcus and Stephen Best's "Surface Reading: An Introduction," 12.

21. Kendrick, 6-7. The term "pretend" might seem to go without saying with regard to novels, but it is especially appropriate when applied to ideology, as a "fantasy-construction which serves as a support for our 'reality' itself" (Žižek, *Sublime*, 45). One might argue further that pretending is akin to wishing: aspiring to a dream-state in which the illusory stands in the place of the real.

22. Žižek again: "The Lacanian definition of a fool is somebody who believes in his immediate identity with himself; somebody who is not capable of a dialectically mediated distance towards himself, like a king who thinks he

is a king, who takes his being-a-king as his immediate property and not as a symbolic mandate imposed on him by a network of intersubjective relations of which he is a part" (*Sublime*, 46). Thomas writes of a "paradigmatic shift in the realm of subjectivity: the replacement of the entire ideologically laden notion of Victorian moral character (something we associate with high realism) with the more physiologically based but socially defined conception of Victorian identity." Thomas, *Detective Fiction*, 63.

23. The classic work on Freud's relation to nineteenth-century narrative is Marcus, *Freud and the Culture of Psychoanalysis*.

24. "An ideology is really 'holding us' only when we do not feel any opposition between it and reality"; Žižek, *Sublime*, 49. The idea that realist novels "feel real" comes from Grenier, *Sympathetic Realism*, 16, 48, and elsewhere.

25. On the classic realist text, see Belsey, 67–84, and MacCabe, 39–45.

26. On thing theory, see Brown, *Things*, and Freedgood.

27. The fetishism of objects or "things" produced by recent theoretical movements such as "thing theory" reinforces, as well, a fetishism of writing, or what Lefebvre has called an "illusion of transparency." "The act of writing is supposed," he suggests, " . . . to imply a discipline that facilitates the grasping of the 'object' by the writing and speaking 'subject.'" Lefebvre, *Production of Space*, 28.

28. Logan, *Victorian Fetishism*, 85.

29. See Daston and Galison. Caroline Levine's discussion of Ruskin's realist aesthetic provides another example; *Serious Pleasures*, 21–25.

30. Armstrong's "an object is never just an object" might be taken as an anticipation of surface reading's idea of "just reading." Writes Bourdieu, "The mind is a metaphor of the world of objects which is itself but an endless circle of mutually reflecting metaphors"; 91. I also want to suggest that certain conventions, such as coincidence, have both a realist life and a fantasy life, in the sense that their presence in ordinary experience seems to violate conventions associated with the real; the argument that coincidence is not "realistic" then becomes an argument for the uniqueness of individual subjectivity.

31. On realism as a mode rather than a genre, see Malik, "We Are Too Menny."

32. Saldivar, "Trollope's *The Warden* and the Fiction of Realism," 169.

33. Eliot, *Middlemarch*, 194.

Chapter 1

1. This is part of Lefebvre's larger argument about abstract space as an effect of capitalist development and organization; Lefebvre cites Guy Debord's account of spectacularization as another example of this emphasis on the

visual. The realist novel, in my reading, is another example of public space, its emphasis on visuality reinforcing its connection to Lefebvre's conception of abstract space. Lefebvre, *Production of Space*, 286.

2. Lefebvre argues that social life from the eighteenth century onward is dominated by "a set of things/signs and their formal relationships: glass and stone, concrete and steel, angles and curves, full and empty. The signification of this ensemble refers back to a sort of super-signification which escapes meaning's net: the functioning of capitalism, which contrives to be blatant and covert at the same time" (49). Though he is chiefly referring to modernism, and, in the epigraph to this chapter, to public space, as Josephine McDonagh points out, many of the characteristics he discusses, including an emphasis on visual display, appear as well in earlier historical periods and in realist representation; she also discusses *Adam Bede* in particular. McDonagh, "Space, Mobility, and the Novel," 50–67. For a discussion of the way writing creates an effect of solidity, see Elaine Scarry, *Dreaming by the Book*, especially chapter 2, "On Solidity," 10–30. I thank Kai Hainer for calling this passage to my attention.

3. Isobel Armstrong writes, of what she calls "window moments" in Victorian novels, that such moments imagine the window as an extension of the body, "the seam, or junction, of the body's internal space." *Victorian Glassworlds*, 115. Remy Saisselin describes the realist novelist's preoccupation with detail, "central to the bourgeois interior," as "the dream world of the bourgeois, his sentimental world of recall, souvenirs, associations, intimate escape from the world of material cares"; *Bourgeois and the Bibelot*, 70–71. For a more historically-oriented interpretation of this novel's frames, see Bowlby, "Two Interventions on Realism."

4. Stewart, *Dear Reader*.

5. The most influential account of these issues remains Belsey's in *Critical Practice*.

6. Deleuze and Guattari, *Thousand Plateaus*, 311–12.

7. Ermarth, *Realism and Consensus*.

8. "There can be no question but that social space is the locus of prohibition, for it is shot through with both prohibitions and their counterparts, prescriptions. This fact, however, can most definitely not be made into the basis of an overall definition, for space is not only the space of 'no,' it is also the space of the body, and hence the space of 'yes,' of the affirmation of life" Lefebvre, *Production of Space*, 201. For Lefebvre, the space of "yes" tends to affirm the body, while the space of "no" disdains, rejects, and prohibits. My argument is that realist space renders the space of yes and the space of no the same.

9. Brown, *Bourgeois Interior*, 62.

10. Fried, *Absorption and Theatricality*, 61.

11. *Adam Bede*'s narrator is often described as masculine, and is aligned with the male gaze because of the quality of attention directed toward Hetty, and "his"

self-designated status as a "friend" of Adam's. My argument aligns the narrator with the author in her relation to realist space.

12. Eliot, "Natural History of German Life."

13. Dinah blushes here under the pressure of Adam's gaze; at the end of the novel, having given up her preaching, her fuller body and ruddier complexion cause her to resemble Hetty even more. There are other suggestions of exchangeability: the double signing of names; Hetty dressed in Dinah's clothes; the scenes in which Adam expects one and gets the other. Dinah's blush has been persuasively read by Margaret Homans as her necessary inscription into bourgeois domesticity. But it may also signify less a change in her than, once again, a re-tooling of readerly perception: the real re-framed so as to register its ability to incite desire. Dinah's blush, that is, suggests the necessary exchangeability of the two women in the context of realist representation, and the necessary complicity of realism's representations in the business of making the real desirable. Unlike Hetty's blush, which radiates for any observer, Dinah's recalls the reflected light of the Vermeer-like domestic scene, reflecting only Adam's gaze and circulating only within the domestic sphere. Homans, "Dinah's Blush, Maggie's Arm."

14. Colomina, *Privacy and Publicity*, 276.

15. See for example Menke, *Telegraphic Realism*, 157.

16. Lukacs, "Bourgeois Interior," 630.

17. Yeazell notes the resemblance of these images to Dutch genre painting; *Art of the Everyday*, 101–102.

18. See O'Farrell, "Provoking George Eliot," 152–54.

19. The usual argument is that Hetty's narcissism isolates her from the community; for a summary of the discussion, see Marck. It is worth noting that the passage I used above to highlight Dinah's interiority is directly preceded by one in which Hetty displays her attention to exteriority and her unsuitedness for domestic labor, as she uses the highly polished surfaces of the Poyser household—the domestic interior—to admire her own reflection: "Hetty Sorrel often took the opportunity, when her aunt's back was turned, of looking at the pleasing reflection of herself in those polished surfaces, for the oak-table was usually turned up like a screen . . . and she could see herself sometimes in the great round pewter dishes that were ranged along the shelves" (73).

20. Scarry, *Body in Pain*, 256; also Bourdieu, "The mind is a metaphor of the world of objects which is itself but an endless circle of mutually reflecting metaphors." *Outline of a Theory of Practice*, 91.

21. I refer here to the moment that an individual becomes a subject, according to Althusser, turning around in response to a policeman's call or "hailing." "Ideology and Ideological State Apparatuses," 174.

22. Bender, *Imagining the Penitentiary*, 65.

23. See McDonagh for a discussion of this issue. Such reproducibility becomes part of the argument, developed throughout this book, that in contrast to its understood emphasis on unique identity and individual subjectivities, realism shares with sensation fiction an unacknowledged reliance on positionality: the significance, recurrence, and stability of social roles over and above the people who fill them.

Chapter 2

1. Felski, "Nothing to Declare," 38.
2. Stone, *Family, Sex, and Marriage*, 29.
3. Steedman, "True Romance," 32.
4. Dickens, *Oliver Twist*, xxxvii–xxxviii.
5. McCrea, *In the Company of Strangers*, 38–39.
6. Paulos, quoted in Neimark, "The Power of Coincidence." The transformation of contingency into meaning affirms, as well, Bourdieu's description of the habitus, which, he writes, "makes coherence and necessity out of accident and contingency." Bourdieu, *Outline of a Theory of Practice*, 87.
7. In other words, fantasy overwhelms the real here: an imagined and wished-for resemblance becomes, for the novel's purposes, a genealogical fact and biological reality.
8. And, it is worth mentioning, without turning him from a major character into a minor one, since major characters are associated with moral, spiritual ideals, with ethereality and non-materiality, while the distinctive characteristics of minor characters ground them in the material world. See Wolloch, *One vs. the Many* for an extended discussion of this issue.
9. When Brownlow sees the portrait next to Oliver, the narrative refers to Oliver's face as "its living copy,—the eyes, the head, the mouth; every feature was the same" (93). This insistence on sameness is to some extent belied by the text's refusal to describe any details of the resemblance; indeed, the catalogue of features—eyes, head, mouth—reinforces the blandness typically attributed to Oliver's physical appearance. To some extent scholarly discussion of the blankness of Oliver's appearance may derive substantially from Cruikshank's drawings, but Dickens's descriptions certainly do not contradict them. The details about the portrait are these: the dying nurse who wishes to confide in Miss Corney says that "The boy grew so like his mother . . . that I could never forget it when I saw his face" (196–97). When Oliver awakens for the first time at Mr. Brownlow's home, he complains of the way the portrait's eyes seem "fixed" on him, as if it "wanted to speak to me, but couldn't" (90). Mr. Brownlow notices a "something" in the boy's face, but "can recall no one countenance of which Oliver's features bore a trace" (80). This inability to discern "one" countenance is perhaps the novel's best account of the issue,

since Mr. Brownlow never met Agnes, Oliver's mother, but knows her appearance only through the portrait done by his friend, Oliver's father. We can add to this Mrs. Bedwin's assertion that "painters always make ladies out prettier than they are, or they wouldn't get any custom," a suggestion reinforced by Oliver's comment that the face in the portrait is "so very pretty: so very beautiful" (90). In what resembles a relay of gazes linking Leeford to Brownlow and mediated by the portrait, the "something" Brownlow recognizes suggests an idealized amalgam of the "looks" of his friend Leeford, Leeford's sister, and Agnes. Brownlow refers to his experience of seeing Oliver thus: "Even when I first saw him, in all his dirt and misery, there was a lingering expression in his face that came upon me like a glimpse of some old friend flashing on one in a vivid dream" (413).

10. "How I Met Your Mother" is an American situation comedy that ran from 2005 to 2014. My argument here relies more on its title and premise than on any particular details of its plot.

11. The look is not only a monitory one, but also a Lacanian one, if one makes use of the idea that the mother's gaze "connects the child's look with the image in the mirror producing the misrecognition that founds his identity." This formulation is Nancy Armstrong's; *Fiction in the Age of Photography*, 24. Oliver's trajectory is, of course, a series of misrecognitions whose end seeks to conceal the fact that the identity the novel finally chooses for him, documented by Brownlow and Monks, is merely another fabrication.

12. These conclusions required some rethinking in light of the series' final episodes, in which a mother is finally revealed but just as quickly killed off. Happily, it turns out that the almost simultaneous bringing-to-existence and doing-away-with the mother figure leaves my conclusion intact: the mother remains, like Oliver's mother, a fantasy figure: very much a "picture" and retrospective construction, whose story is only told to her children six years after her death. She is wholly idealized, while her death leaves Ted to continue (in the imaginations of now-bereft viewers) his quest for romantic fulfillment.

13. Dickens, *Great Expectations*, 498

14. Wahrman, *Imagining the Middle Class.*

15. For a related discussion of exchange in this novel, see Abravanel, "Hardy's Transatlantic Wessex."

16. This would be a version of realist disillusionment, in which maturity is defined as a recognition that the aspirations of youth must give way to "the more narrow confines of a circumscribed and relatively common individual life." Moretti, *Way of the World*, 35.

17. Hardy, *The Mayor of Casterbridge*, 322.

18. Howe, "The Struggles of Men," 384.

19. Convention's historicity appears in Abravanel's comparison of the wife-sale to slavery, which conforms to a certain historical rule of "what is done," as, according to Hardy, does wife-selling more generally in medieval times. Abravanel, "Transatlantic"; Hardy, 379.

20. "The incidents narrated arise mainly out of three events . . . in the real history of the town called Casterbridge. . . . They were the sale of a wife by her husband, the uncertain harvests which immediately preceded the repeal of the Corn Laws, and the visit of a Royal personage to the aforesaid part of England" (379). See Thompson, "The Sale of Wives," 404–66, for a historical account of wife-selling.

21. See Sarah Winter's account, via Joel Kovel, of this kind of relation between psychology and capitalism: "Kovel argues that seeing one's fate as a product of the psychological struggles of the 'inner self' means that the social, economic, and political causes of human suffering under advanced capitalism cannot be perceived and therefore cannot come under the kind of political pressure that might help to generate social change." Winter, *Freud*, 16.

22. "In sleep there come to the surface buried genealogical facts, ancestral curves, dead men's traits, which the mobility of daytime animation screens and overwhelms" (124).

23. See Woloch for discussions of the relation between novelistic position and social space, specifically with respect to "minority" status.

24. Farfrae is himself represented as secondary, an imitation of a type.

25. On the idea of the counterfactual, see A. Miller, "Lives Unled."

Chapter 3

1. Trollope, *Orley Farm*, I:398.

2. Bailin, *Sickroom in Victorian Fiction*, 9. This formulation resembles one that Jameson describes in Proust, "in which the object to be fantasized is magically evoked by way of its very renunciation." The realist text, or what Jameson calls here the "Symbolic text"—as opposed to the Imaginary one, which is more easily satisfied—"seeks to endow itself with the utmost representable density and to posit the most elaborate and systemic difficulties and obstacles, in order the more surely to overcome them." Jameson, *Political Unconscious*, 183.

3. See Ch. 5 for a discussion of the dream as genre.

4. Allen writes of this habit, "it was a form of play and a substitute for the play with others that he had been denied. It also took a specific form and one not usually ascribed to adolescents: it was bound by distinct narrative principles, and especially those of fictional realism. In other words, he was mentally practicing a specific form of fiction." "Trollope to His Readers," 13.

5. J. Hillis Milller has discussed what he calls the "masturbatory" resonance of Trollope's language in the first passage, suggesting that though Trollope's "official" theory was that the novels made the "dangerous" material of the daydreams safe for public consumption, they in fact retained their subversive sexual content. Miller, *Ethics of Reading*; see also Allen, "Masculinity and

Novel-Writing." For a detailed analysis of the *Autobiography*'s use of fantasy and fairy-tale narrative strategies, see Gilead, "Trollope's *Autobiography*."

6. Kendrick, *Novel-Machine*, 87–88; Anderson, "Trollope's Modernity," 509; Richardson, "Competitive World"; Poovey, "Trollope's Barsetshire Series," 41. A more general context for this discussion would include recent discussions of the way characters in Victorian novels think, including A. Miller, *Burdens of Perfection*; Hadley, *Living Liberalism*, 63–124, and Pinch, *Thinking about Other People in Nineteenth-Century British Writing*.

7. Shaw, review of Jane Nardin, *Trollope and Moral Philosophy*, 358.

8. Dames, "Trollope and the Career," 252.

9. This is a version of, though not exactly the same as, Leo Bersani's argument that the realist novel expels its desiring heroes and heroines. My argument to some extent echoes his observation that "Realistic fiction depends on the distinctness of those boundaries [between illusion and reality], and yet the first great realistic novel [Cervantes's *Don Quixote*] takes curious risks in an occasionally indecisive play with the elements meant to stand for the real and those meant to stand for delusion." Bersani, *Future for Astyanax*, 68.

10. See also Stephen Wall on Trollope's "photographic" realism. Herbert, *Trollope and Comic Pleasure*, 189; Wall, "Trollope, Satire, and *The Way We Live Now*".

11. The idea that Trollopian fantasy remains within the boundaries of the real might seem to contradict Jenny Bourne Taylor's argument, and Trollope's own suggestion (after his remark about Collins: "A good novel should be both, and both in the highest degree"), that he is sensational as well as realistic. Certainly, Trollope shares with sensation fiction an interest in legal transgressions, property laws, and courtroom scenes involving powerful and attractive women; certainly his fiction sometimes registers bodily intensities in a "sensational" manner. My point is not to quibble about generic boundaries or to claim that there is no mixing of genres in Trollope's fiction. But to say, as Bourne Taylor does, that Trollope adds "social and psychological concerns" to sensational plot structures does not adequately account for the texture of his realism, which, however sensational the plot, always includes characters' extended introspection about the steps they are taking. More, the number of scenes of characters simply sitting and thinking in *Orley Farm* alone directly opposes the speeded-up narrative of sensation fiction: if anything, the novel tests a reader's willingness to watch a character sitting in almost complete stillness, as Peregrine Orme does, sometimes with the barest train of thought to follow, sometimes with none. ("There was a silence between the host and his guest for some two or three minutes, during which Mr. Mason was endeavouring to get the lunch out of his head, and to redirect his whole mind to Lady Mason and his hopes of vengeance. There is perhaps nothing so generally consoling to a man as a well-established grievance;

a feeling of having been injured, on which his mind can brood from hour to hour, allowing to plead his own cause in his own court, within his own heart,—and always to plead it successfully" [I:81]. "She sat there perfectly still for nearly an hour, and during the whole of that time there was the same look of agony on her brow. Once or twice she rubbed her hands across her forehead, brushing back her hair, and showing, had there been anyone there to see it, that there was many a gray lock there mixed with the brown hairs.... She knew that her enemies were conspiring against her,—against her and against her son; and what steps might she best take in order that she might baffle them?" [I:46]. "Lady Mason sat there perfectly still for about an hour thinking what she would do" [I:47]. "It was clear to Mr. Furnival that even Mr. Round junior would be glad that it should pass off. And then he also sat thinking" [I:248]. "That her mind was full of thoughts I need hardly say, but yet the hour seemed very long to her" [I:265].) Bourne Taylor, "Trollope and the Sensation Novel," 87 et passim.

12. The term "narratable" is D. A. Miller's; *Narrative and Its Discontents*.

13. Trollope, *Warden*, 34.

14. Trollope, *Barchester Towers*, 325.

15. Trollope, *The Way We Live Now*, 96.

16. This process resembles, though it is not identical to, what Nicholas Dames has called Trollope's "career" narrative, which is cumulative, presenting "a sequence of tutelary examples whose full meaning can only be known once the entire sequence has been consumed and all the examples are present to compare with one another." "Trollope and the Career," 253–54. My account of speculation and thinking as labor fits as well with Franco Moretti's description of prose as work, or what he also calls *rationalizing the novelistic universe*: turning it into a world of few surprises, fewer adventures, and no miracles at all." "Serious Century," 381–82; italics in original.

17. Barthes, "The Reality Effect."

18. In this sense, what I am describing resembles what Carolyn Dever calls "microplots," though the ultimate justification for her is the building of suspense. While I agree that Trollope embeds "narrative tension within individual psyches that are tested by the uncertain expectations of social modernity," my sense is that the proliferation of possibilities is not primarily about building suspense and is in many ways anti-suspense. Dever, "Trollope, Seriality, and the 'Dullness' of Form," 863. Caroline Levine argues that suspense enhances novelistic realism by making readers "speculate and hypothesize ... pause in the knowledge that we do not know"; Levine, *Serious Pleasures of Suspense*, 3. What I am calling castles in the air differ from the suspenseful narratives she describes, however, and the judgments readers are called upon to render about characters or events in my account are not the same as (in her argument) the discovery of facts about the empirical world.

19. There are echoes in this account of Alexander Bain's description of the novel as "the literature of pursuit," as in this account of the novel reader: "On the physical side, the situation of pursuit is marked by the intent occupation of one or other of the senses, accompanied with a fixed attitude generally. . . . The fixed stare of the eye, the alertness of the ear, the groping touch, are well known manifestations. . . . According as we are engrossed by things beyond ourselves, self-consciousness is in abeyance; and if the engrossment attains an extreme pitch, there is an almost entire suspension of feeling or emotion." Bain, *Emotions of the Will*, 1852, quoted in Dames, *Physiology of the Novel*, 44. Dames focuses on Bain's definition of the novel via the nature of its readers, so that the genre is seen not as a construction of language but rather as "*a mode of cognitive activity*" (45; emphasis in original). Chapter Two of Dames's book discusses Victorian scenes of reading and reverie, both absorptive and distracted.

20. Trollope, *Dr. Wortle's School*, 28.

21. Dever, 863; also Bourne Taylor.

Chapter 4

1. Hardy, *Return of the Native*, 387.

2. Hardy, *Jude the Obscure*, 88–90.

3. On Hardy's memory-infused landscapes, see Barrell, "Geographies of Hardy's Wessex"; Irwin, *Reading Hardy's Landscapes*: and J.H. Miller, *Topographies*.

4. Hardy has often been called an "anti-realist"; see for example Levine, *Realistic Imagination*, 229–51, and Shires, "Radical Aesthetic." Mitchell, however, calls him "a representative of high realism"; "Hardy's Female Reader," 174.

5. The term "landscape" ordinarily refers to something external and at least ostensibly natural. My use of it here relies, first of all, on the idea that representations may and do blur differences between one sort of "reality" and another; and, second, on what I believe is the as-yet-unacknowledged way in which the theoretical analysis of landscape, as discussed here, overlaps with that of literary realism.

6. In the 1912 Preface to *Far from the Madding Crowd,* Hardy famously asked his readers not to try to imagine Wessex characters outside of Wessex. *Far from the Madding Crowd*, 393.

7. "The mirror . . . transforms what I am into the sign of what I am." Lefebvre, *Production of Space*, 185. The window, in this case, functions like a mirror, and the sign-system into which Clym projects himself discloses whether he is included or excluded—part of the community or, as I suggest below,

of the general atmosphere of his native place—or not. As Jill Matus notes, metonymy is also tied to absence: "The metonymic effect is an indefinite linear extension of the subject's search and lack"; "Proxy and Proximity," 317. Noting the use of the term "screen" as a metaphor for the function of windows and cinema, Anne Friedberg discusses Stanley Cavell's description of the screen as a barrier: "As an action verb," she writes, "the screen renders the spectator invisible, keeps the spectator from the world it holds in its frame." Friedberg, *Virtual Window*, 17.

8. Eliot's pier-glass, like mirrors in other Victorian novels, suggests some distortion of what is nevertheless taken to be the "real"—as in the reflection of Bertha Mason in Jane Eyre's mirror in Brontë's novel. But reflection in such cases, unlike those I discuss here, is susceptible to explanations that are plausible both psychologically and in terms of realist conventions.

Each of the framing structures mentioned here (mirrors, windows, and walls) has its particular epistemological and metaphorical status, and it is not my purpose either to conflate them or to differentiate in detail between them. The flat planes of both suggest their similar function as barriers, while the translucency, transparency, and/or reflective qualities of windows and mirrors are sometimes interchangeable, sometimes not. Hardy uses both, however, to divide space into apparently distinct ontological registers—realities that are simultaneously the same and not the same—as well as to suggest the fantasmatical properties that, it follows, may attach to the space in which we tend to find them, the conventional bourgeois home.

9. My emphasis on the materialization of conventions in Hardy bears some resemblance to Elaine Scarry's description of "the material record of the interaction between man and world" in his work, though her emphasis is on the way traces left by labor render the invisible visible, dissolving boundaries between character and world. Scarry, *Resisting Representation*, 52.

10. For a contrasting argument see Shires, "Radical." D.A. Miller writes of *Middlemarch*: "We are familiar with how, in life, various perspectives of an object come to be 'proof' of its reality; how, in novels generally, different views of a character may suggest the depth of a full existence." Miller, *Narrative and Its Discontents*, 128.

11. Žižek, "Psychoanalysis and the Lacanian Real," 222. An extended discussion of this idea appears in Žižek, *Sublime*, 1–56.

12. While Alberti's glass was not the plate glass of Hardy's time, he used the idea of glass to help him visualize the arrangement of points on a transparent or translucent plane. Friedberg emphasizes the idea that the key element for Alberti was not the glass but the frame, though he does refer to a surface "transparent and like glass" (Friedberg, 29). The absence of transparency in Alberti's glass—what Freidberg calls "translucency"—brings the metaphor

of the window closer to that of a barrier or wall, at the same time maintaining its suggestiveness as a surface that is at least somewhat visually porous.

13. Roberts distinguishes between MacCabe's view, which he dubs "classic realism," and "classical realism," which both "adopts and subverts the dominant conditions of bourgeois specularity." MacCabe, *Tracking the Signifier*, 39; Roberts, "Realism, Modernism, and Photography," 163.

14. Relevant here is Lefebvre's notion of reciprocity, in which individual and environment are seen as mutually constitutive. *Production of Space*, 183–89.

15. Hardy, *Woodlanders*, 128.

16. The impossibility of this image—of proving, disproving, or indeed reproducing it—puts it in the realm of the "virtual," as Anne Friedberg defines that term. Friedberg discusses two meanings of virtuality: "an image produced in the brain without reference in the world," and "an image produced out of some optical mediation." Both, she writes, "imply a separate ontological register, an immaterial form that is *functionally but not effectively* material" (italics in original). "This meaning of 'virtual' suggests an intangible, uncapturable, ineffable appearance—more *imago* than *pictura*" (9). Though the eye here does appear in the mirror—a surface "placed in its plane"—its unverifiability and the terms of its description, distancing it from the subject reflected and locating it fantasmatically in the minds of both characters, suggest the aptness of this idea of virtuality. Marjorie Levinson discusses a similar detached eye in Hardy's poetry (573) and in relation to the drawing of his glasses. Levinson, "Object-Loss and Object-Bondage," 571. Also relevant here is Isobel Armstrong's discussion of the way nineteenth-century "glass culture" disperses and deflects reflections of the self; *Victorian Glassworlds*, especially 95–103.

17. In Hardy's drawing, the glasses are an image of the landscape's "floating eyes." They are not eyes, however, but two-way surfaces: windows and walls. Without earpieces, Levinson suggests, one cannot tell which way they are facing, but the solid frame on the left seems to answer that question. Ostensibly positing a necessary one-way perspective (the world will look "real" when viewed through the glasses the "correct" way, not the reverse), the glasses also invite the viewer to imaginatively walk around them and peer in the other way: to look in as an outsider, as well as out as an insider.

18. "Not to be hailed is to feel a draining of subjectivity and desire" (Roberts 159). In *Le systeme des objects*, writes Lefebvre, Jean Baudrillard sees the mirror as nothing more, for the bourgeois, than "an extension of 'his' drawing-room or bedroom" (185). Hardy's mirrors and other framed surfaces, such as Clym's window, repudiate this role: they reflect neither the bourgeois room nor the subjectivity projected by it but rather the question of the subject's relation to it, his or her status as insider or outsider. "Wessex" functions overall as the opposite of this bourgeois mirror: it refuses to let us in; it refuses to comfort us; it refuses especially the knowable distinction between inside and outside on which bourgeois comfort and realist representation rely.

19. Says Fitzpiers to Giles, "You are right enough if you imagine that I am in love with something in my own head" (115). Fitzpiers's reading includes relevant references to Fichte, or what George Levine calls "watered down German philosophy": "There's only Me and Not Me in the whole world." Hardy, *Woodlanders*, 47; Levine, *"Woodlanders* and the Darwinian Grotesque," 190.

20. "Consider a window. Is it simply a void traversed by a line of sight? No. In any case, the question would remain: what line of sight—and whose? The fact is that the window is a non-object which cannot fail to become an object. As a transitional object it has two senses, two orientations: from inside to outside, and from outside to inside. Each is marked in a specific way, and each bears the mark of the other" (Lefebvre 209). The flexibility of "a woman's face at the window" echoes "the eye of the reflected image": both are detached, both belong to no one in particular.

21. This is of course a psychological reading, in which the drama acts out Clym's unconscious desires. But it is also a social one, in which houses and the marriages that go with them are inherently boundary-creating insitutions, designed to include some and exclude others.

22. The "primitiveness" of this space is important because it hovers, as do other windows, mirrors, and walls throughout Hardy's work, between materiality and metaphor. The hut is little more than an enclosure, its walls suggesting both the boundary of marriage and the "correctness" that keep Giles and Grace away from one another. Like skin, the walls of the hut perform the basic function of keeping the outside out and the inside in.

23. Goode, *Hardy*, 94, 107.

24. As Grace explains, "You know what I feel for you—what I have felt for no other living man, what I shall never feel for a man again! But as I have vowed myself to somebody else than you, and cannot be released, I must behave as I do behave, and keep that vow" (307).

25. Levinson describes a similar structure in Hardy's poetry in relation to the psychoanalytic idea of introjection, in which "the young child mentally takes in the object, usually the mother, in the form of an *imago* (a whole-person form) so as to ensure its constant availability, to protect it, to preserve it, and also, to repudiate whatever is experienced as bad or dangerous about it" (561–62). Here, Clym might be said to simultaneously introject his mother and imagine his introjection by her.

26. This formulation resembles Shires's suggestion that Hardy is committed to a form of "not knowing," or not choosing: that he has an "ability to hold multiple points of view at once and not [have to] choose or hierarchise among them." Shires, "Unknowing Omniscience," 36.

27. Recall MacCabe's comment, cited above: "The real is not articulated: it is." Also relevant here is Jessica Benjamin's account of the projective nature of certain representations of women, as in the townspeoples' identification of

Eustacia as a witch: "The usage of *she is* . . . signifies a collapse of reality and fantasy." Benjamin, "The Omnipotent Mother," 132–33.

28. On Clym's metonymic connection to his surroundings and connections between body and landscape more generally in Hardy, see Cohen, 99–102. J.Hillis Miller describes the relation between character and landscape in this novel as "catachresis"; *Topographies*, 27–28. On metonymy and proximity, see Matus.

29. To use buildings or other objects as "stimulants" for one's own aspirations is, in effect, to transform the world into a novel: to perceive abstract space as a vehicle for one's desires.

30. Clym's creeping and winged familiars are more of him than about him, their own "nativeness" reinforced by the idea that they are "never seen elsewhere."

31. In his 1895 preface to *Far from the Madding Crowd* (393). In a different vein but in a manner not unconnected to the dynamic of inviting exclusion discussed here, Genevieve Abravanel has argued that Wessex's (and in particular, Casterbridge's) isolation is both a response to "the threat of transatlantic commodification and exchange" and a strategy for "marketing rural Englishness for American consumption." Abravanel, "Hardy's Transatlantic Wessex," 113.

Chapter 5

1. Collins, *Armadale*, 710.

2. Henry Mansel famously linked sensation fiction to newspapers, writing of the sensation-fiction author: "Let him only keep an eye on the criminal reports of the daily newspapers, marking the cases which are honoured with the especial notice of a leading article, and become a nine-days' wonder in the mouths of quidnuncs and gossips; and he has the outline of a story not only ready-made, but approved beforehand as of the true sensation cast." "Sensation Novels," 495. Collins himself recognized the potential value for his work of the growing "mass" of readers, whom he numbered somewhere in the "three millions," and with whom the future of English fiction, he noted, may rest. Collins, "Unknown Public," 217–22. Sensation novels typically drew on murder and bigamy cases; Collins's attention to news of *The Armadale* differs both in kind and in temporal relation (the news following the novel, as he points out). For a brief discussion of the appendix, including Richard Altick's citation of the relevant newspaper article, see *Armadale*, 710.

3. The appendix also functions as a third ending, following the two Jenny Bourne Taylor describes. Bourne Taylor, *"Armadale."* Matthew Rubery discusses novels' use of newspaper material, including shipwrecks, in *The Novelty of Newspapers*, Ch. 2.

4. And they are indeed unstable, especially "realism" and the idea of the real. Sensation fiction, of course, is allied with realism in its desire to give the lie to bourgeois respectability, and relies on the shock value of real-world behavior rather than on what Collins might call "supernatural" events. *Armadale*'s suffocation scenes are in some sense realistically plausible, but they also draw on and arouse, as I will argue here, a primal, nightmarish scenario associated more closely with dream and fantasy than with sensation fiction's usual scandals.

5. *Armadale* has proven generally resistant to criticism. At the close of his argument about the novel's logic of exchange, Nathan Hensley discusses the "abstracting" moves his argument has compelled him to make; "*Armadale* and the Logic of Liberalism," 627. Both he and Bourne Taylor remark that whatever one says about this sprawlingly complex novel necessarily leaves a great deal out, with numerous details remaining unabsorbed into any larger critical framework. This argument is no exception. And yet if I can offer the following without it seeming too much like an excuse, the novel's own appeals to dream logic as well as its emphasis on the extensively mediated quality of any knowledge that provides, within it, a basis for action or direction, suggests an opposition to realism that is both thematic and methodological as well as ideological: an attempt to resist the stable account that a realist text, and perhaps a sensationalist one as well, is expected to offer.

6. My point is not that this is a quality limited to realist fiction: all fiction, we might hazard, establishes an internal framework of events that are said, in the fictional universe, to have actually happened; these events become the structure in relation to which other events may be deemed fantastical.

7. In Žižek's and Lacan's terms, this mirroring skirts the traumatic kernel the dream approaches but cannot quite represent. The novel's representation of the real is dreamlike despite its realist claim; in the everyday life we awaken to, Žižek writes, we are "*nothing but a consciousness of this dream*" (48; italics in original). *Armadale*'s use of this scene at the novel's beginning and end also suggests a mirroring effect, the trauma of the end recalling, in dreamlike fashion, the novel's pre-history.

8. See Bourne Taylor.

9. Later, we learn that Armadale recognizes his father in his own dream because of a picture he has seen of him.

10. The issue of whether the facts of ordinary life are disputed or not is my own addition, not an aspect of Freud's argument. My point is that these details serve as anchors, the idea of the real called upon, once again, to stabilize and render comprehensible what might otherwise seem inexplicable.

11. The retrospective quality this analysis posits also suggests that the dream temporally distorts the external event. For even as the stimulus or irritant may seem to provoke, counter-intuitively, the dream it appears to follow,

the pinpointing of a stimulus such as an alarm clock's ring or a noise in the street also reveals the dream's actual duration to be much briefer than the dreamer's experience suggests. I return to this issue at the end of the chapter.

12. See Freud for a discussion of this issue in relation to Maury's dream. The argument here is that a "ready made fantasy" is provoked by a stimulus, the fantasy itself not in fact dreamed but recalled upon awakening. The idea that the past is an effect of the future—that a particular event's meaning, or indeed existence, may be revealed or become apparent only in retrospect, as an effect of new knowledge—is what Freud called *Nachtraglichkeit* or deferred action, and Jean Laplanche, more recently, "afterwardsness." Freud, *Interpretation of Dreams*, 533–36; Laplanche, "Notes on Afterwardsness." My thanks to Kent Puckett for the Laplanche reference.

13. Though sensation fiction was frequently described as a herald of social and moral decline, it was also described as a "sign of the times," offering a depiction of people and events readers might encounter any day; see Mansel's *Quarterly Review* essay. In *Lady Audley's Secret* (1863), Mary Elizabeth Braddon offers murders committed in the country as a representation of what goes on behind the placid surface of rural life. See *Lady Audley's Secret*, 51.

14. The "undreamlike" quality of this representation is an instance of this text's sophisticated deployment of the conventions of genre: the way in which, at numerous points, Collins destabilizes the categories on which readers, and its own internal interpreters, will rely to make sense of the narrative. In the rigidity of its attention to process—the numbering of each "plot point"—it also prefigures Freud's claim that the waking consciousness constructs coherent narrative out of the incoherence of dreams (351).

15. The source of the pools and lakes of the dream's landscape is, Midwinter suggests, a newspaper account of "Travels in Australia" which Allan had been recently reading; the "original" of the image of his father ("How did you know that the figure appearing to you in the dream was the figure of your father?") turns out to have been a portrait—a miniature "found on the floor of the cabin" (188). The dream, thus understood, mediates mediation or perhaps exposes it, transforming the already transformed or perhaps exaggerating its transformative effects. The "real" to which it ties us is itself mediated: like the newspaper report, reworking not the event itself but a report or image. The dream's transformation is thus itself secondary, a reworking of already reworked material.

16. Collins's appendix is also highly mediated: in offering up this anecdote, he includes as proof of its veracity two newspaper accounts, "in which I can cite the dates—in *The Times* of November 30th, 1865 . . . more fully described in the *Daily News* of November 28th in the same year" (662). He thus at

once makes the novel into a predictive dream and invests the predictive dream with something of the status of the real: what had seemed unlikely or impossible—at the very least, bizarre—turns out to be true.

17. Thomas, *Detective Fiction*. This emphasis on position participates in and continues the critique of realist identity—the idea that individual identity is essential and indispensable—undertaken by Hardy in *The Mayor of Casterbridge*. Positionality is also a key concept in Freudian dream interpretation and in psychoanalysis in general, since interpretations often rely on the idea that individuals imaginatively occupy more than one position in any given scene.

18. Is "Armadale" a person, a place, or, as Collins's appendix tells us, a ship? Is there one Armadale, or many? Does "Armadale" name a single, unique individual, or does it signify numerous persons, and hence suggest the possibility of interchangeability? In this latter sense, the strangeness of the name has a purpose. For while one might expect to encounter many Davids or Janes, an "Armadale" would seem unique—and encountering more than one even more peculiar. In fact, there are two towns named Armadale: one on the Isle of Skye in Scotland, and another in Western Australia. It seems not to be known generally as a person's name in these places or anywhere else.

19. As Nathan Hensley argues, beyond the exchangeability of the two Armadales who are the novel's chief subjects lies the potential interchangeability of persons in general.

20. Of course, the most conventional element of the conventional love story is that "It had to be you"—that the beloved is unique and irreplaceable. One might point here toward Bashwood, who is left at the novel's end in the grip of "his favourite delusion," waiting at the church for his beloved Lydia to arrive and marry him: "perfectly harmless, and perfectly happy" (659).

21. It might sound as if I am evoking the Lacanian idea, discussed in my introduction, that there are three realms: the real, fantasy, and the Real. Rather, I maintain that the capital-R real relies on the term for its power, and that dreams are no more characterized by "real" content than waking life. These are all genres, including the real, its ideological tenor emphasized here by the way the theory of dream interpretation invoked turns the external world into a minefield in which any domestic glitches may have major, potentially life-threatening consequences.

In a *New Yorker* article about the idea of collecting dreams on the Internet so as to establish a dream archive, Hunter Lee Soik is quoted as follows: "You can speak or text a dream. If you speak, it will transcribe the audio, then we'll run an algorithm through the dream and pull out all the keywords. 'Horses,' 'airplanes,' 'red cars,' 'running,' 'jumping.'" My point is simply that it is possible to come up with the "keywords" only if one has a sense in advance of what constitute the dream genre: of the characteristic shape one expects a dream to have. Throughout *Interpretation*, Freud seeks to interpret his conclusions about individual dreams as discoveries "of general validity" (175); this is, indeed, the purpose of the book. Wilkinson, "Brave New World Dept.," 24.

Chapter 6

1. Best and Marcus, "Surface Reading."
2. Daston and Galison, "Image of Objectivity," 120.
3. Hayles, "How We Read," 12; 17.
4. Freedgood and Schmitt, "Denotatively, Technically, Literally."
5. The best critique of surface reading I have encountered is Cannon Schmitt, "Tidal Conrad (Literally)." But the alternative he articulates, situated in a compelling reading of "Heart of Darkness," relies like the surface-reading manifesto on a rhetoric of clear vision: the definition of the ebb tide he provides allows us to "envision with precision what happens in the first part of 'Heart of Darkness'" (18), while terms such as "ships, masts, and sails," he argues, in their denotative function render details of the text "instantaneously clear to readers possessed of specialized knowledge. The task is to make them clear to all readers and then consider their function or effect in light of that clarity" (16). I would argue, however, not only that the power Schmitt attributes to denotation manifests a desire for the real, but also that once such terms are framed within a literary text—in this instance "Heart of Darkness"—they lose their literal status. The tide imagined as a "restraint" on human action is not a literal tide but one that has been anthropomorphized (25). In this sense the literal—like the "real" I discuss throughout this book—is once again imagined as a binding or prohibitive force, specifically one that binds language to its object.
6. Darwin, *Expression of the Emotions*, 188.
7. Both of these examples exemplify what Ruth Leys has described as an attempt to capture the real in the form of what takes place when no one is looking; in this sense they also resemble my account of omniscience in *Dombey and Son*. The ostensibly neutral, invisible stance of Trollope's narrator—classically staged in relation to a woman's privacy, both as she is situated logistically (in her own room) and in her activity (expressing emotion she will not show in public) is echoed by Darwin's relation to the woman on the train. The "accidental" nature of his discovery of her aligns her with an object of chance observation in the natural world, reinforcing the likelihood that she is only one of many similar instances of the same phenomena, while the absence from his discussion of the possible effect of his own presence

on what he observes similarly suggests that as he is effectively not there. See Leys, "How Did Fear"; Jaffe, *Vanishing Points*, 71–110.

8. Woolf, "Mr. Bennett and Mrs. Brown," 29.

9. This discussion recapitulates, in different form, issues about the type versus the individual that appear in Gallagher, "George Eliot," and that I discuss in *Affective Life of the Average Man*.

WORKS CITED

Abravanel, Genevieve. "Hardy's Transatlantic Wessex: Constructing the Local in *The Mayor of Casterbridge*." *Novel* 39 (2005): 97–117.

Allen, Peter. "Masculinity and Novel-Writing in Trollope's *An Autobiography*," *Prose Studies* 16 (1993): 62–83.

————. "Trollope to His Readers: The Unreliable Narrator of *An Autobiography*." *Biography* 19 (1996): 1–18.

Althusser, Louis. *Lenin and Philosophy and other Essays*. Translated by Ben Brewster. New York: Monthly Review Press, 1971.

Anderson, Amanda. "Trollope's Modernity," *ELH* 74 (2007): 509–34.

Armstrong, Isobel. *Victorian Glassworlds: Glass Culture and the Imagination 1830–1880*. Oxford: Oxford University Press, 2008.

Armstrong, Nancy. *Fiction in the Age of Photography: The Legacy of British Realism*. Cambridge: Harvard University Press, 1999.

————. *How Novels Think: The Limits of Individualism from 1719–1900*. New York: Columbia University Press, 2005.

Arnold, Matthew. *Culture and Anarchy*. Edited by Jane Garnett. Oxford: Oxford University Press, 2009.

Bailin, Miriam. *The Sickroom in Victorian Fiction: The Art of Being Ill*. Cambridge: Cambridge University Press, 1994.

Barrell, John. "Geographies of Hardy's Wessex." *Journal of Historical Geography* 8 (1982): 347–61.

Barthes, Roland. "The Reality Effect." In *The Rustle of Language*. Translated by Richard Howard. Oxford: Blackwell, 1986, 141-48.

————. *S/Z*. Translated by Richard Miller. New York: Hill and Wang, 1974.

Batchelor, Rhonda. Review of Laurie Langbauer, *Novels of Everyday Life*. *Victorian Review* 25 (2000): 118–21.

Belsey, Catherine. *Critical Practice*. London: Methuen, 1980.

Bender, John. *Imagining the Penitentiary: Fiction and the Architecture of Mind in Eighteenth-Century England*. Chicago: University of Chicago Press, 1987.

Benjamin, Jessica. "The Omnipotent Mother: A Psychoanalytic Study of Fantasy and Reality." In *Representations of Motherhood*, edited by Donna Bassin, Margaret Honey, and Maryle Mahrer Kaplan, 129–46. New Haven: Yale University Press, 1994.

Bersani, Leo. *A Future for Astyanax: Character and Desire in Literature*. Boston: Little Brown, 1976.

Best, Stephen, and Sharon Marcus. "Surface Reading: An Introduction." Representations 109 (2009): 1–21.

Bourdieu, Pierre. *Outline of a Theory of Practice*. Translated by Richard Nice. Cambridge: Cambridge University Press, 1991.

Bowlby, Rachel, "Introduction: Two Interventions on Realism." *Textual Practice* 25 (2011), 396–436.

Braddon, Mary Elizabeth. *Lady Audley's Secret*. Edited by Lyn Pykett. Oxford: Oxford University Press, 2012.

Brooks, Peter. *Realist Vision*. New Haven: Yale University Press, 2005.

Brown, Bill, ed. *Things*. Chicago: University of Chicago Press, 2004.

Brown, Julia Prewitt. *The Bourgeois Interior: How the Middle Class Imagines Itself in Literature and Film*. Charlottesville: University of Virginia Press, 2008.

Christoff, Alicia. "Alone with *Tess*," *Novel* 48 (2015): 18–44.

Collins, Wilkie. *Armadale*. Edited by John Sutherland. New York: Penguin, 1995.

———. "The Unknown Public." *Household Words* 18 (1858): 217–22.

Colomina, Beatriz. *Privacy and Publicity: Modern Architecture as Mass Media*. Cambridge: MIT Press, 1996.

Dames, Nicholas. *The Physiology of the Novel: Reading, Neural Science, and the Form of Victorian Fiction*. New York: Oxford University Press, 2007.

———. "Trollope and the Career: Vocational Trajectories and the Management of Ambition." *Victorian Studies* 45 (2003): 247–78.

Darwin, Charles. *The Expression of the Emotions in Man and Animals*. Edited by Paul Ekman. New York: Oxford University Press, 1998.

Daston, Lorraine, and Peter Galison. "The Image of Objectivity." *Representations* 40 (1992): 81–128.

———. *Objectivity*. Cambridge: MIT Press, 2010.

Deleuze, Gilles, and Felix Guattari. *A Thousand Plateaus: Capitalism and Schizophrenia*. Translated by Brian Massumi. Minneapolis: University of Minnesota Press, 1987.

Dever, Carolyn. "Trollope, Seriality, and the 'Dullness' of Form." *Literature Compass* 7/9 (2010): 861–66.

Dickens, Charles. *Great Expectations*. Edited by David Trotter. London: Penguin, 1997.

———. *Oliver Twist*. Edited by Philip Horne. London: Penguin, 2003.

Eliot, George. *Adam Bede*. Edited by Valentine Cunningham. New York: Oxford University Press, 1996.

———. *Middlemarch*, Edited by Rosemary Ashton. London: Penguin, 1994.

———. "The Natural History of German Life." *Westminster Review* (1856), 51–79.

Ermarth, Elizabeth. *Realism and Consensus in the English Novel*. Princeton: Princeton University Press, 1983.

Felski, Rita. "Nothing to Declare: Identity, Shame, and the Lower Middle Class." *PMLA* 115 (2000): 33–45.

Freedgood, Elaine. *The Ideas in Things: Fugitive Meaning in the Victorian Novel*. Chicago: University of Chicago Press, 2006.

———. "The Novelist and Her Poor." *Novel* 47 (2014): 210–23.

Freedgood, Elaine, and Cannon Schmitt. "Denotatively, Technically, Literally." *Representations* 125 (2014): 1–14.

Fried, Michael. *Absorption and Theatricality: Painting and Beholder in the Age of Diderot*. Berkeley: University of California Press, 1980.

Friedberg, Anne. *The Virtual Window: From Alberti to Microsoft*. Cambridge: MIT Press, 2006.

Freud, Sigmund. *The Interpretation of Dreams*. Translated by James Strachey. New York: Basic Books, 1965.

Gallagher, Catherine. "George Eliot: Immanent Victorian." *Proceedings of the British Academy* 94 (1996): 157–72.

Gilead, Sarah. "Trollope's *Autobiography*: The Strategies of Self-Production." *Modern Language Quarterly* 47 (1986): 272–90.

Goode, John. *Thomas Hardy: The Offensive Truth*. Oxford: Blackwell, 1988.

Grenier, Rae. *Sympathetic Realism in Nineteenth-Century British Fiction*. Baltimore: Johns Hopkins University Press, 2012.

Hadley, Elaine. *Living Liberalism: Practical Citizenship in Mid-Victorian Britain*. Chicago: University of Chicago Press, 2010.

Hardy, Thomas. *Far from the Madding Crowd*. Edited by Shannon Russell and Rosemarie Morgan. New York: Penguin, 2003.

———. *Jude the Obscure*. Edited by Dennis Taylor. New York: Penguin, 1998.

———. *The Mayor of Casterbridge*. Edited by Keith Wilson. New York: Penguin, 2003.

———. *The Return of the Native*. Edited by Simon Gatrell. New York: Oxford University Press, 2005.

———. *The Woodlanders*. Edited by Patricia Ingham. New York: Penguin, 1998.

Hayles, N. Katherine. "How We Read: Close, Hyper, Machine." *ADE Bulletin* 150 (2010): 62–79.

Hensley, Nathan. "*Armadale* and the Logic of Liberalism." *Victorian Studies* 59 (2009): 607–32.

Herbert, Christopher. *Trollope and Comic Pleasure*. Chicago: University of Chicago Press, 1987.

Homans, Margarett. "Dinah's Blush, Maggie's Arm: Class, Gender, and Sexuality in George Eliot's Early Novels." *Victorian Studies* 36 (1993): 155–70.

Howe, Irving. "The Struggles of Men." In *Thomas Hardy's The Mayor of Casterbridge*, edited by Phillip Mallet, 384–98. New York: Norton, 2000.

Irwin, Michael. *Reading Hardy's Landscapes*. London: Palgrave McMillan, 2000.

Jaffe, Audrey. *The Affective Life of the Average Man: The Victorian Novel and the Stock-Market Graph*. Columbus: Ohio State University Press, 2010.

———. *Vanishing Points: Dickens, Narrative, and the Subject of Omniscience*. Berkeley: University of California Press, 1991.

Jakobson, Roman. "Metaphoric and Metonymic Poles." In *Roman Jakobson, Selected Writings*, edited by Stephen Rudy. Vol. II. The Hague: Mouton, 1971.

Jameson, Fredric. *The Antinomies of Realism*. London: Verso, 2013.

———. *The Political Unconscious: Narrative as a Socially Symbolic Act*. Ithaca: Cornell University Press, 1981.

Kendrick, Walter. *The Novel-Machine: The Theory and Fiction of Anthony Trollope*. Baltimore: Johns Hopkins University Press, 1980.

Langbauer, Laurie. *Novels of Everyday Life: The Series in English Fiction*. Ithaca: Cornell University Press, 1999.

Laplanche, Jean. "Notes on Afterwardsness." In *Essays on Otherness*, edited by John Fletcher, 261–65. New York: Routledge, 1999.

Lefebvre, Henri. *The Production of Space*. Translated by Donald Nicholson-Smith. Malden, MA: Blackwell, 1974.

Levine, Caroline. *The Serious Pleasures of Suspense: Victorian Realism and Narrative Doubt*. Charlottesville: University of Virginia Press, 2003.

Levine, George. *The Realistic Imagination*. Chicago: University of Chicago Press, 1981.

———. "*The Woodlanders* and the Darwinian Grotesque." In *Thomas Hardy Reappraised: Essays in Honor of Michael Millgate*, edited by Keith Wilson, 174–98. Toronto: University of Toronto Press, 2006.

Levinson, Marjorie. "Object-Loss and Object-Bondage: Economies of Representation in Hardy's Poetry." *ELH* 73 (2006): 549–80.

Leys, Ruth. "How Did Fear Become a Scientific Object, and What Kind of Object Is It?" *Representations* 110 (2010): 66–104.

Logan, Peter. *Victorian Fetishism: Intellectuals and Primitives*. New York: SUNY University Press, 2009.

Lukacs, John. "The Bourgeois Interior." *The American Scholar* 39 (1970): 616–30.

Lynch, Deidre. *The Economy of Character: Novels, Market Culture, and the Business of Inner Meaning.* Chicago: Unversity of Chicago Press, 1998.

MacCabe, Colin. *Tracking the Signifier.* Minneapolis: University of Minnesota Press, 1985.

Macherey, Pierre. *A Theory of Literary Production.* London: Routledge, 1978.

Malik, Rachel. "We Are Too Menny." *New Left Review* 28 (2004): 139–49.

Mansel, Henry. "Sensation Novels." *Quarterly Review* (April 13, 1863): 495–96.

Marck, Nancy Ann. "Narrative Transference and Female Narrators: The Social Message of *Adam Bede.*" *Studies in the Novel* 35 (2003): 447–70.

Marcus, Steven. *Freud and the Culture of Psychoanalysis.* London: Allen & Unwin, 1984.

Matus, Jill. "Proxy and Proximity: Metonymic Signing." *University of Toronto Quarterly* 58 (1998–1999): 305–26.

Matz, Aaron. *Satire in an Age of Realism.* Cambridge: Cambridge University Press, 2010.

McCrea, Barry. *In the Company of Strangers.* New York: Columbia University Press, 2011.

McDonagh, Josephine. "Space, Mobility, and the Novel: 'The spirit of place is a great reality.'" In *Adventures in Realism,* edited by Matthew Beaumont, 50–67. Malden, MA: Blackwell, 2007.

Menke, Richard. *Telegraphic Realism: Victorian Fiction and Other Information Systems.* Stanford: Stanford University Press, 2008.

Miller, Andrew. "Lives Unled in Realist Fiction." *Representations* 98 (2007): 118–234.

———. *The Burdens of Perfection: On Ethics and Reading in Nineteenth-Century British Literature.* Ithaca: Cornell University Press, 2008.

Miller, D. A. *Narrative and Its Discontents: Problems of Closure in the Traditional Novel.* Princeton: Princeton University Press, 1989.

———. *The Novel and the Police.* Berkeley: University of California Press, 1988.

Miller, J. Hillis. *The Ethics of Reading: Kant, deMan, Trollope, James, and Benjamin.* New York: Columbia University Press, 1987.

———. *Topographies.* Stanford: Stanford University Press, 1995.

Mitchell, Judith. "Hardy's Female Reader." In *The Sense of Sex: Feminist Perspectives on Hardy,* edited by Margaret Higonnet, 173–87. Champaign: University of Illinois Press, 1993.

Moretti, Franco, "Serious Century." In *The Novel,* Vol. 2., edited by Franco Moretti, 364–400. Princeton: Princeton University Press, 2007.

———. *The Way of the World: The Bildungsroman in European Culture.* New York: Verso, 1987.

Neimark, Jill. "The Power of Coincidence." *Psychology Today*, July 1, 2004. https://www.psychologytoday.com/articles/200407/the-power-coincidence.

Newsom, Robert. *A Likely Story: Probability and Play in Fiction*. Newark, NJ: Rutgers University Press, 1988.

O'Farrell, Mary Ann. "Provoking George Eliot." In *Compassion: The Culture and Politics of an Emotion*, edited by Lauren Berlant. New York: Routledge, 2004.

Pendarvis, Jack. "The Fifty Greatest Things That Just Popped into My Head." *The Believer Magazine* (2009): 76–77.

Pinch, Adela. *Thinking about Other People in Nineteenth-Century British Writing*. Cambridge: Cambridge University Press, 2013.

Poovey, Mary. "Trollope's Barsetshire Series." In *The Cambridge Companion to Anthony Trollope*, edited by Carolyn Dever and Lisa Niles, 31–43. Cambridge: Cambridge University Press, 2011.

Richardson, Rebecca. "A Competitive World: Ambition and Self-Help in Trollope's *An Autobiography* and *The Three Clerks*." *The Fortnightly Review* (2012): np.

Roberts, John. "Realism, Modernism, and Photography." In *Adventures in Realism*, edited by Matthew Beaumont, 158–76. Malden, MA: Blackwell, 2007.

Rubery, Matthew. *The Novelty of Newspapers: Victorian Fiction after the Invention of the News*. New York: Oxford University Press, 2009.

Saisselin, Remy. *The Bourgeois and the Bibelot*. Newark, NJ: Rutgers University Press, 1984.

Saldivar, Ramón. "Trollope's *The Warden* and the Fiction of Realism." *Journal of Narrative Technique* 11 (1981): 166–83.

Scarry, Elaine. *Dreaming by the Book*. Princeton: Princeton University Press, 1999.

——. *Resisting Representation*. New York: Oxford University Press, 1994.

——. *The Body in Pain: The Making and Unmaking of the World*. New York: Oxford University Press, 1984.

Schor, Hilary. *Curious Subjects: Women and the Trials of Realism*. New York: Oxford University Press, 2013.

Schmitt, Cannon. "Tidal Conrad (Literally)." *Victorian Studies* 55 (2012): 7–29.

Shaw, David. Review of Jane Nardin, *Trollope and Moral Philosophy*. *Victorian Studies* 40:2 (1997): 358.

Shires, Linda. "The Radical Aesthetic of *Tess of the D'Urbervilles*." In *The Cambridge Companion to Thomas Hardy*, edited by Dale Kramer, 145–63. Cambridge: Cambridge University Press, 1999.

——. "The Unknowing Omniscience of Hardy's Narrators." In *Thomas Hardy Texts and Contexts*, edited by Thomas Mallett, 31–48. London: Palgrave, 2002.

Smajic, Srdan, "Supernatural Realism." *Novel* 42 (2009), 1–22.

Steedman, Carolyn. "True Romance." In *Patriotism: The Making and Unmaking of British National Identity*, Vol. I, edited by Raphael Samuel, 26–35. Cambridge: Cambridge University Press, 1991.

Stewart, Garrett. *Dear Reader: The Conscripted Audience in Nineteenth-Century British Fiction*. Baltimore: Johns Hopkins University Press, 1996.

Stone, Lawrence. *The Family, Sex, and Marriage in England 1500–1800*. New York: Harper & Row, 1977.

Taylor, Jenny Bourne. "*Armadale*: The Sensitive Subject as Palimpsest." In *Wilkie Collins: Contemporary Critical Essays*, edited by Lyn Pykett, 149–74. New York: St. Martin's Press, 1998.

———. "Trollope and the Sensation Novel." In *The Cambridge Companion to Anthony Trollope*, edited by Carolyn Dever and Lisa Niles, 85–98. Cambridge: Cambridge University Press, 2010.

Thomas, Ronald. *Detective Fiction and the Rise of Forensic Science*. Cambridge: Cambridge University Press, 2004.

Thompson, E. P. *Customs in Common*. New York: New Press, 1993.

Trollope, Anthony. *An Autobiography*. Edited by Michael Sadleir and Frederick Page. Oxford: Oxford University Press, 1999.

———. *Barchester Towers*. Edited by Robin Gilmour. London: Penguin, 1983.

———. *Dr. Wortle's School*. Edited by John Halperin. New York: Oxford University Press, 1984.

———. *Orley Farm*. Edited by David Skilton. New York: Oxford University Press, 1985.

———. *The Warden*. Edited by David Skilton. New York: Oxford University Press, 1980.

———. *The Way We Live Now*. Edited by Frank Kermode. London: Penguin, 2002.

Wall, Stephen. "Trollope, Satire, and *The Way We Live Now*." *Essays in Criticism* (1987): 43–61.

Warman, Drohr. *Imagining the Middle Class: The Political Representation of Class in Britain, c. 1780–1840*. Cambridge: Cambridge University Press, 1995.

Watt, Ian. *The Rise of the Novel*. Berkeley: University of California Press, 1957.

Weinstein, Philip. *Unknowing: The Work of Modernist Fiction*. Ithaca: Cornell University Press, 2005.

Wilkinson, Alec. "Brave New World Dept.: Dream On." *The New Yorker* (October 28, 2013):24.

Winter, Sarah. *Freud and the Institution of Psychoanalytic Knowledge*. Stanford: Stanford University Press, 1999.

Woloch, Alex. *The One vs. the Many: Minor Characters and the Space of the Protagonist in the Novel*. Princeton: Princeton University Press, 2003.

Woolf, Virginia. "Mr. Bennett and Mrs. Brown." In *Essentials of the Theory of Fiction*, edited by Michael J. Hoffman and Patrick D. Murphy, 24–39. Durham: Duke University Press, 1966.

Yeazell, Ruth. *Art of the Everyday: Dutch Painting and the Realist Novel.* Princeton: Princeton University Press, 2008.

Žižek, Slavoj. "Psychoanalysis and the Lacanian Real: 'Strange shapes of the unwarped primal World." In *Adventures in Realism*, edited by Matthew Beaumont, 207–23. Malden, MA: Blackwell, 2007.

———. *The Sublime Object of Ideology.* New York: Verso, 1989.

INDEX

CPSIA information can be obtained
at www.ICGtesting.com
Printed in the USA
BVHW082350020519
547148BV00001B/4/P